Dear Maria
Hope you find
something to laugh
about everyday!
Blessings or Your ador...
Jor, Ayjier ad...
Psalm '26...
love,

THE
ALL AMERICAN
JOKE BOOK

By BOB PHILLIPS

HARVEST HOUSE PUBLISHERS
Eugene, Oregon 97402

Dedicated to all of the brilliant connoisseurs of great humor who have the outstanding intelligence and courage to buy my fourth joke book . . . and to my good wife Pam who laughs at her husband's jokes, not because they are clever, but because she is.

THE ALL AMERICAN JOKE BOOK

Copyright © 1976 Harvest House Publishers
Eugene. Oregon 97402 Library of Congress Catalog Card
Number: 75-34744 ISBN-0-89081-016-8

[Printed in the United States of America]

TABLE OF CONTENTS

INTRODUCTION

Not long ago a friend asked, "Why are you writing another joke book? You have already written THE WORLD'S GREATEST COLLECTION OF CLEAN JOKES, MORE GOOD CLEAN JOKES, and THE LAST OF THE GOOD CLEAN JOKE BOOKS." I explained to him it was because of a phone call I received from my publisher.

A few months earlier my publisher called and told me he had some "Good News." He informed me that they had just sold my millionth joke book. I was so excited that I hung up the phone and ran to my typewriter and began compiling THE ALL AMERICAN JOKE BOOK. As I was on the last chapter of this new joke book, my publisher called again and said that he had some "Bad News." He told me that it was true that they had sold my millionth joke book, but they still hadn't been able to get rid of the first 999,999 joke books.

I then decided to help promote the sales by going on a speaking tour. I remember the first (and last) banquet I spoke at. I was so nervous and bit my nails so much that my stomach needed a manicure. With great skill I told a few of the more exciting jokes. Everyone in the audience was on the edge of their seats. Later I found out they were trying to muster the nerve to get up and go home. I told the audience that my joke books would be read long after Milton and Homer have been forgotten. Someone in the back of the room yelled, "And not until then!" The master of ceremonies then leaned over to the man next to him and I heard him say, "His humor is like history . . . it repeats itself." I ignored their lack of good taste and knew that, at least, the news media would give me tremendous reviews.

The next day I looked in the paper for an article about the banquet the night before. I couldn't find a thing. I was a little upset and called the editor of our local newspaper. I said, "I thought your paper was friendly to me?" "So it is," replied the editor. "What's the matter?" "Well," I went on, "you did not print even one of my jokes that I told at the banquet last night." The editor replied, "Man, what further proof of our friendliness do you want?"

Realizing that I would have a hard time selling my first three joke books, I turned all my energies toward the printing of THE ALL AMERICAN JOKE BOOK. I sent the manuscript to one publisher and got no reply. Finally, I called his secretary. I asked her if her boss had read my latest book. She told me that he had gotten a side ache over my manuscript. I said, "Oh, really. Did he find it that amusing?" She said, "No. He had just fallen asleep on top of it."

I decided the only way to sell the new manuscript was to go to a publisher in person. After nine days of waiting I finally got in to see him. I selected the best jokes and began reading them to him. Two minutes later I woke him up and said, "How could you sleep when I was reading my jokes to you. You knew how much I wanted your opinion." "Young man," replied the editor, "Sleep **is** an opinion."

"But," I responded, "there must be some channel THE ALL AMERICAN JOKE BOOK could get in to?" He suggested the English Channel. "You see," the publisher went on to say, "the trouble with the publishing business is that too many people who have half a mind to write a book do so." He thought that the only way my jokes would get in front of an audience would be if they were ground up and used as confetti.

Even though the various publishers have offered such kind words of encouragement . . . coupled with the fact that as a result of writing the first three joke books, there have been four assassination attempts . . . and 312 threats on my life in the last three months . . . I will not give up. I am continually spurred on by (something) and the thought that "all work and no plagiarism makes a dull joke book."

If you can't laugh at these jokes in THE ALL AMERICAN JOKE BOOK . . . all you have to do is put them in the stove and I know that you will hear the fire roar.

—Bob Phillips

CAMPUS COMEDIANS

Teacher: You missed school yesterday, didn't you?
Student: Not a bit.

• •

Teacher: Give, for one year, the number of tons of coal shipped out of the United States.
Student: 1498; None.

• •

It was a bright spring morning and four high school boys decided to skip school. They arrived at school after lunch and told the teacher that their car had a flat tire along the way and that was why they were late.

To their relief, the teacher smiled and said: "You boys missed a little test this morning. Please take seats apart from one another and get out your paper and pencil."

When the boys were seated the teacher said, "Each of you please answer just one question. Which tire was flat?"

• •

Sign in school cafeteria: SHOES ARE REQUIRED TO EAT IN THE CAFETERIA
Someone wrote below: SOCKS CAN EAT WHEREVER THEY WANT

• •

In the old days if a college student went to the dean's office it meant the student was in trouble. Today it means the dean is in trouble.

• •

If the cost of education continues to rise, education will become as expensive as ignorance.

• •

Teacher: I am dismissing you ten minutes early today. Please go out quietly so as not to wake the other classes.

• •

Mike: Did you knock'em cold in the Latin quiz?
Bill: Yes, zero.

• •

Teacher: In which of his battles was King Alexander the IXV of Smogaria slain?
Student: I'm pretty sure it was the last one.

• •

Teacher: What is the axis of the earth?
Student: The axis of the earth is an imaginary line which passes from one pole to the other, and on which the earth revolves.
Teacher: Very good. Now, could you hang clothes on that line?
Student: Yes, sir.
Teacher: Indeed, and what sort of clothes?
Student: Imaginary clothes, sir.

• •

A college education never hurt anyone who was willing to learn something afterwards.

• •

Teacher: We borrowed our numerals from the Arabs, our calendar from the Romans, and our banking from the Italians. Can anyone think of other examples?
Student: Our lawn-mower from the Smiths, and our ladder from the Wilsons.

• •

2

Teacher: Can you give me a good example of how heat expands things and cold contracts them?
Student: Well the days are much longer in the summer.

• •

Teacher: Now remember, students, statistics don't lie. Now, for an example, if twelve men could build a house in one day, one man could build the same house in twelve days. Do you understand what I mean?
Student: You mean that if one boat could cross the ocean in six days, six boats could cross the ocean in one day.

• •

Teacher: And who is the Speaker of the House?
Student: Mother.

• •

I am reminded of the faculty member who wouldn't move into his new living quarters when he learned it was just a stone's throw from the campus.

• •

Student: It's going to be a real battle of wits, I am now a member of the debating team.
Roommate: How brave of you to go unarmed.

• •

Student: Yes, sir, I always carry my notes in my hat.
Teacher: I see . . . knowledge in a nutshell.

• •

Teacher: What was George Washington famous for?
Student: He was chiefly famous for his memory.
Teacher: What makes you think his memory was so great?

Student: Because they erected a monument to Washington's memory.

• •

History teacher: How many of you object to war? (Many hands shot up.) Mark, tell me why you object to war.
Mark: 'Cause wars make history.

• •

Teacher: Were you copying his paper?
Student: No, sir, I was only looking to see if he had mine right.

• •

Teacher: Where is the elephant found?
Student: It's so big, it's hardly ever lost.

• •

First student: Let's cut philosophy today.
Second student: I can't. I need the sleep.

• •

Rosie: What is your brother in college?
Nancy: A half-back.
Rosie: I mean in his studies.
Nancy: Oh, in his studies he's away back.

• •

Professor: Do you enjoy Dickens' novels?
Student: Oh, yes I do. Every time another one comes out I go right down to the store and buy it.

• •

I stood in the corner so much in school that I had a triangular forehead.

• •

Teacher: Johnny, name a great time saver.
Johnny: Love at first sight.

• •

I went to high school so long that the other students brought me apples . . . they thought I was the teacher.

• •

A college education costs from eight to ten thousand dollars. That's a lot of money to invest and only get a quarter back.

• •

Teacher: Do you know what Neoplatonism is?
Student: That's easy. Strawberry, chocolate and vanilla ice cream.

NOURISHMENT

Customer: Look here, waiter, is this peach or apple pie?
Waiter: Can't you tell from the taste?
Customer: No, I can't.
Waiter: Well, then, what difference does it make?

• •

I've always wanted to spend money lavishly, but I certainly never thought it would be on sugar, milk, bread and mayonnaise.

• •

Customer: Bring me two poached eggs on toast, and mince pie with plenty of powdered sugar on it.
Waiter: (Shouting to cook) Adam and Eve on a raft . . . a hunk of everything, and let it come in a snowstorm.

• •

A very plump man spooning up a banana split said to his friend, "I'm counting calories. So far today I've had 9716."

• •

Woman in supermarket: Give me thirty cents worth of potatoes, please.
Grocer: Why don't you take a whole one?

• •

Sign in restaurant: OCCUPANCY NOT TO EXCEED 150. PLEASE HELP US GET A VIOLATION.

• •

First Cannibal: Have you seen the dentist?
Second Cannibal: Yes. He filled my teeth at dinner.

• •

Cannibal Cook: Shall I stew both those cooks we captured?
Cannibal King: No; one is enough. Too many cooks spoil the broth.

• •

Customer: Don't you think this steak you served me is a little thin?
Waiter: Don't be silly. If the steak was any thicker, you couldn't see the picture on your plate.

• •

A bachelor was eating breakfast in a restaurant when he saw the following note written on an egg: "Should this meet the eye of some young man who desires to marry a farmer's daughter, age 19, write . . . ."

The bachelor wrote and in a few days received the following note: "Your letter came too late. I am now married and have four children."

• •

Man to headwaiter: Can you see that we get a table near the sugar bowl.

BIBLE RIDDLES

Question: When did Ruth treat Boaz badly?
Answer: When she pulled his ears and trod on his corn.

• •

Question: What is the difference between Noah's Ark and an Archbishop?
Answer: One was a high ark, but the other is a hierarch.

• •

Question: How do we know that Noah had a pig in the ark?
Answer: He had Ham.

• •

Question: Can you spell "Adam's Express Company" with three letters?
Answer: E-V-E.

• •

Question: Where did Noah strike the first nail in the ark?
Answer: On the head.

• •

Question: Why was Moses the most wicked man who ever lived?
Answer: He broke the Ten Commandments all at once.

• •

Question: If Solomon was the son of David and Joab was the son of Zeruiah, what relation was Zeruiah to Joab?
Answer: His mother.

• •

Question: Who was Jonah's tutor?
Answer: The fish that brought him up.

· ·

Question: In what place did the cock crow when all the world could hear him?
Answer: In Noah's Ark.

· ·

Question: How did the fish that swallowed Jonah obey the divine law?
Answer: Jonah was a stranger, and he took him in.

· ·

Question: How many neck-ties did Job have?
Answer: Three wretched comforters.

· ·

Question: Who was the fastest runner in the world?
Answer: Adam, because he was first in the human race.

· ·

Question: What did Adam and Eve do when they were expelled from Eden?
Answer: They raised Cain.

· ·

GIVE THEM THE BUSINESS

A salesman walked into a diner and taking his place on one of the vacant stools, ordered bread and milk. The fellow sitting on the next stool asked:

"On a diet?"

"No. Commission."

· ·

Customer: What do you mean! Seven hundred dollars for that antique! Last week you only wanted four hundred and fifty dollars.
Dealer: Well, you know how the cost of labor and materials keeps going up.

•   •

Joe: I can't understand why you failed in business.
Moe: Too much advertising.
Joe: You never spent a cent in your life on advertising.
Moe: That's true, but my competitor did.

•   •

A salesman mentioned that he'd only gotten three orders for an entire week's worth of work: Get out. Stay out. And don't come back.

•   •

When a salesman was told by a customer that a competitor offered the same merchandise for less money he replied, "I have no quarrel with anyone who sells for less. After all, they ought to know what their merchandise is worth."

•   •

A boss called the entire office staff together and told them a new joke. Everyone but one man laughed uproariously. "What's the matter?" grumbled the boss. "Don't you have a sense of humor?"

"I don't have to laugh," said the man. "I'm leaving Friday anyhow."

•   •

Sign in store: TRY OUR EASY PAYMENT PLAN. ONE HUNDRED PERCENT DOWN. NOTHING ELSE TO PAY.

•   •

The following note was given to all the employees of a large workshop: "Whenever I enter the workshop I want to see every man cheerfully performing his task. Therefore, I invite you to place in the Suggestion Box any suggestions as to how this can be brought about. Signed: The Boss."

A week later the box was opened; it contained only one slip of paper, on which was written: "Don't wear rubber heels."

•   •

He is a born executive . . . his father owns the business.

•   •

A customer was several months behind in paying his bill and his last payment notice informed him that he would have to pay or the matter would be turned over to a lawyer. He responded with the following note: "Enclosed you will find a check for the entire amount. Please forgive my delay in not answering sooner. Thank for your patience. I remain, Yours Truly . . ."

"P.S. This is the kind of a letter I would write you if I had the money to pay."

•   •

Mankind is divided into two classes: those who earn their living by the sweat of their brow, and those who sell them handkerchiefs, cold drinks and electric fans.

•   •

A personnel manager in a large company kept a goldfish on his desk. He said it was nice to have something around that opened its mouth without asking for a raise.

•   •

A salesman was summoned to the office to discuss his oversized expense account.

"How in the world," asked the manager, "do you manage to spend $30.00 a day for food?"

"It isn't hard," came the reply. "I skip breakfast."

• •

Employer: Personal appearance is a helpful factor in business success.

Employee: Yes, and business success is a helpful factor in personal appearance.

• •

A large store was crowded with customers waiting for attention. All of a sudden the phone rang and a voice asked if a certain item was in stock. "Just a moment," the clerk said, and returned with the news that the item was in stock. "That will be $15.95 C.O.D. To what name and address shall we send it?"

"Never mind sending it," said the voice on the telephone. "Just bring it to the front of the store . . . I'm in the public telephone booth there."

• •

A customer was talking to the complaint department clerk refunding money on a returned item: "But you're not refunding it cheerfully."

• •

President: Is our advertising getting results?

Vice President: It sure is. Last week we advertised for a night watchman and the next night we got robbed.

• •

Irate Buyer: This car you sold me won't even climb a hill! You said it was a fine machine!

Dealer: I said: 'On the level it's a good car.'

• •

If the paper clip were invented today, it would probably have ten moving parts, five transistors and require a service man three times a year.

• •

Did you hear about the man who went to pick up his film at one of those photo-processing stores? The clerk told him it was not ready. The man said, "Your sign said 24-Hour Service." "Oh, that's true," said the clerk. "But that means three eight-hour days."

• •

Customer: If it only costs $15.00 to make these watches, and you sell them for $15.00, where does your profit come in?
Shopkeeper: That comes from repairing them.

• •

Young man: May I ask you the secret of your success?
Executive: There is no easy secret, you just jump at your opportunity.
Young man: But how can I tell when my opportunity comes?
Executive: You can't, you have to keep on jumping.

• •

City man: Which is correct? To say a hen is 'setting' or 'sitting?'
Farmer: That don't interest me a-tall. What I want to know when I hear a hen cackle is whether she be 'laying' or 'lying.

• •

A hotel guest was awakened at an unearthly hour by a bellboy hammering on his door announcing he had a letter for him.

"Put it under the door," shouted the annoyed guest.

"I can't," came the reply. "It's on a tray."

* *

A good executive is a man who will share the credit with the man who did all the work.

* *

When your automobile engine develops a knock, changes are it's opportunity knocking . . . for some mechanic.

* *

A motorist, after being bogged down in a muddy road, paid a passing farmer five dollars to pull him out with his tractor. After he was back on dry ground he said to the farmer, "At those prices, I should think you would be pulling people out of the mud night and day."

"Can't," replied the farmer. "At night I haul water for the hole."

* *

Sign in sporting goods store: SALE ON TENNIS BALLS—FIRST COME, FIRST SERVE.

* *

An efficiency expert is one who can tell you how to run your business but who isn't smart enough to start his own.

* *

Boss: What's this big item on your expense account?
Salesman: That's my hotel bill.
Boss: See that you don't buy any more hotels.

* *

A man traveling through the country stopped at a small fruit stand and bought some apples. When he commented they were awfully small the farmer replied, "Yup."

The man took a bite of one of the apples and exclaimed, "Not very flavorful, either."

"That's right," said the farmer. "Lucky they're small ain't it."

• •

One reason that Americans will never go communistic is that when they hear the shout, "Workers arise!", they think it's time for the coffee break.

• •

Striker's picket sign: TIME HEALS ALL WOUNDS. TIME AND A HALF HEALS THEM FASTER!

• •

Boss: The main thing to remember is that repetition, repetition, repetition is the keynote! If you have a product to sell, keep harping on it every possible way, cram it down people's throats . . . make yourself sickening and repulsive if you have to, but don't ever forget to repeat and repeat and repeat! It's the only way to get results!
Employee: Yes, sir.
Boss: And now, what was it you came in to see me about?
Employee: Well, sir, a raise! A raise! A raise! A raise! A raise ! A raise! A raise! A raise . . .

• •

Executive: Get my broker, Miss Jones.
Secretary: Yes, sir. Stock or pawn?

• •

Customer: I want to buy a toy train for my little boy.

Clerk: Next floor, please, sir. Men's Hobbies.

• •

The trouble today with staying home from work is that one has to drink coffee on his own time.

• •

Bank President: Where's the cashier?
Manager: Gone to the races.
Bank President: Gone to the races in business hours?
Manager: Yes, sir, it's his last chance of making the books balance.

• •

First Archaeologist: I still don't understand how the ancient Egyptians managed to build the pyramids.
Second Archaeologist: They didn't take coffee breaks.

• •

Manager: What's the customer's complaint this time?
Clerk: It's not a complaint, sir. He wants two shoes that squeak in the same key.

• •

Applicant: Before I take this job, tell me, are the hours long?
Employer: No, only 60 minutes each.

• •

Customer: What do you do when someone forgets his change?
Cashier: I rap on the window with a dollar bill.

• •

The most frustrating occupation in the world must be an elevator operator. He never gets to hear the end of a good story.

• •

Lady: Can you give me a room and bath?
Clerk: I can give you a room, madam, but you will have to take your own bath.

• •

If coffee breaks get much longer, employees will be late for quitting time.

• •

Husband: (Reading the morning paper) Another cup of coffee!
Wife: Aren't you going to the office today?
Husband: Oh, my goodness. I thought I was at the office!

• •

Supervisor: Young lady you are fifteen minutes late on your first day of work.
Employee: Oh no, sir, I just took my coffee break before I came in.

• •

Have you heard about the new "Welfare Doll?" You wind it up and it doesn't work.

• •

First clerk: What a day/ I only sold one dress yesterday, and today is even worse.
Second clerk: How could it be worse?
First clerk: Today the lady returned the dress she bought yesterday.

• •

"I'm very sorry, said the personnel manager, "but if I let you take two hours for lunch today, I'd have to do the same thing for every employee whose wife gave birth to quadruplets."

• •

The postal service is so bad that even letters addressed to "Occupant" are getting lost.

• •

The purchasing agent faces his toughest decision when he negotiates to buy the machine designed to replace him.

• •

Be thankful for the problems, for if they were less difficult, someone with less ability would have your job.

• •

Householder: Well, I see you brought your tools with you.
Plumber: Yeah, I'm getting more absent-minded every day.

BEGGARS

"Please give a poor old blind man a dollar," whined the ragged person at the kitchen door.

"Poor old blind man," said the lady, "why you can see out of one eye."

"Well, then, give me fifty cents."

• •

A tramp accosted a gentleman in the street and asked him for the price of a night's lodging. The gentlemen searched through his pockets only to find that he had no small change, so he said:

"I'm very sorry, but I haven't got the quarter you require in change, but if you'll wait here for a few minutes, I have a few purchases to make up the street, and I'll be back by with some small change."

The tramp considered this for a moment, stroking his whiskers. Then he said:

"That's very good of you indeed; but, sir, you ain't got any idear how much money I lose by giving credit."

•   •

The hobo with the wooden leg had been admitted to the kitchen, and he was dividing his time between the meal that had been set before him and the cook who stood looking on.

"And how did you lose yer leg my good man," asked the cook.

"I was a sailor, mum."

"A sailor?"

"Yes, mum, and one day I fell over the side of the ship and a shark he come along and grabbed me by the leg."

"Merciful hivins," gasped the cook. "And what did you do then?"

"Let him have the leg, o' course, mum. I never argues with sharks."

•   •

First bum: How did that sausage we had at the last place agree with you?
Second bum: I don't know, but I think it hurt my liver wurst.

•   •

Housewife: You should be ashamed to be seen begging in this town.
Hobo: Oh, I don't know. I've seen worse.

•   •

A tramp knocked on the door of the inn known as St. George and the Dragon. The landlady opened the door, and the tramp asked, "Could you give a poor man something to eat?"

"No!" replied the woman, slamming the door in his face.

A few minutes later the tramp knocked again. The landlady came to the door again. This time the tramp asked, "Could I have a few words with George?"

•   •

A panhandler approached a prosperous-looking man and asked for a dime for a cup of coffee. "Is this all you have to do?" replied the man. "Look at you . . . you sleep on park benches, your clothes are tattered, and you're hungry. Why don't you get a grip on yourself and go to work?"

"Go to work!" growled the bum in disgust. "What for . . . to support a bum like me?"

WOMEN'S LIB

The war between the sexes will never be one. There's too much fraternizing with the enemy.

•   •

A girl involved with the Women's Lib movement boarded a crowded bus and one man rose to his feet.

"No, you must not give up your seat . . . I insist," she said.

"You may insist as much as you like, lady," was the reply; "This is my street where I get off."

•   •

A man celebrates his birthday by a day off. A woman takes a whole year off.

•   •

Never praise a woman too highly. If you stop, she'll think you don't love her anymore. If you keep it up, she'll think she's too good for you.

•   •

A women's lib speaker was addressing a large group and said, "Where would man be today if it were not for woman?"

She paused a moment and looked around the room.

"I repeat, where would man be today if it were not for woman?"

From the back of the room came a voice, "He'd be in the Garden of Eden eating strawberries."

• •

A Women's Lib speaker was rudely heckled by a man, who said, "Don't you wish you were a man?"

To which the lady responded, "Don't you?"

• •

I wish the Women's Libbers would hurry through the period when they've ceased being ladies and haven't yet become gentlemen.

• •

Did you hear about Glena Zimmerman? She got involved in the Women's Lib movement and changed her name to Glena Zimmerperson.

• •

A man who traveled to Iran was telling a large audience about how careless the men over there are with their wives. He said it was not an uncommon sight to see a woman and a donkey hitched up together.

From the back of his audience a woman's voice was heard to say, "That's not so unusual . . . you often see it over here, too."

• •

Joe: Do you believe in clubs for women?
Moe: Yes, if every other form of persuasion fails.

• •

If a man makes a stupid mistake, men say: "What a fool that man is."

If a woman makes a stupid mistake, men say: "What fools women are."

• •

Actually, the so-called weaker sex is the stronger sex because of the weakness of the stronger sex for the weaker sex.

• •

Waitress: How many lumps in your tea, sir?
Customer: I'll take mine smooth, please.

• •

Waiter: Would you mind settling your bill, sir? We're closing now.
Customer: But I haven't been served yet.
Waiter: Well, in that case, there'll only be the cover charge.

• •

Customer: Waiter, will you bring me another sandwich, please.
Waiter: Will there be anything else?
Customer: Yes, a paperweight. My first sandwich blew away.

• •

Some people put on weight only in certain places . . . pizza parlors, bakeries, ice cream shops . . .

• •

Housewife: These eggs are very small.
Grocer: Straight from the farm this morning, madam.
Housewife: That's the trouble with these farmers . . . they're so anxious to get their eggs sold they take them off the nest too soon.

• •

Indian: Did you slice'em ham on this sandwich?
Waiter: Yes, I sliced the ham.
Indian: Ugh, you almost missed'em.

•   •

A young woman buying stamps at the post office dropped a letter. The envelope fell directly in front of the gentleman standing next to her. He politely raised his hat. Then he kicked the envelope over in front of her, making it easier for her to pick it up.

•   •

Whenever you hear some fellow say he can read women like a book, it's safe to bet the guy is too old to start a library.

•   •

When a woman repulses, beware. When a woman beckons, bewarer.

•   •

A second grade teacher tells us that the Women's Lib movement is reaching down into the grade schools. The girls refuse to answer questions when Dick has more apples than Jane.

•   •

An authority on words states that an airplane should always be referred to as "she." Does this apply also to mail planes?

•   •

They keep saying that women are smarter than men, but did you ever see a man wearing a shirt that buttoned down the back?

•   •

GOLFERS

A golfer and his caddy argued about which club to use on a short hole. Instead of the recommended No. 3 iron, the golfer used his driver and hit a shot that sliced sharply to the right, hit a tree, bounced back across the green where it struck a rock and caromed . . . yes, you guessed it . . . right into the hole.

Amid whoops of joy, the happy golfer turned to the caddy and said, "See, I told you that was the right club."

•   •

Husband: Sweetheart, I have a present for the person I love best in all the world.
Wife: A set of golf clubs, no doubt.

•   •

As the player holed out on the 18th for a score well over 100, he turned to his caddy and said, "I'll never be able to hold my head up again."

"Oh, I don't know, sir," came the ready reply. "You've been doing it all afternoon."

•   •

A group of golfers were telling tall stories. At last came a veteran's turn. "Well," he said, "I once drove a ball, accidentally of course, through a cottage window. The ball knocked over an oil lamp and the place caught on fire."

"What did you do?" asked his friends.

"Oh," said the veteran, "I immediately teed another ball, took careful aim, and hit the fire alarm on Main Street. That brought out the fire engine before any damage was done."

•   •

Golf is a game where when you don't succeed, you try, try again. And, if you're honest, you mark it down on the score card.

• •

When you putt well, you are a good putter. But when the other fellow is putting well, he has a good putter.

• •

Man blames fate for other accidents, but feels personally responsible when he makes a hole in one.

• •

One golfer was overheard to say to the other, "You know, the closest I ever came to a hole-in-one was 13."

• •

Golfer: Funny game, golf.
Caddy: 'Tain't meant to be.

• •

And of course you know the one about the dentist who refused to make an appointment with a patient because of a busy afternoon.

"I've got 18 cavities to fill," he said as he picked up his golf bag and left his office.

• •

"It's a dirty lie!" said the golfer as he came upon his ball which had fallen right into the middle of a mud hole.

• •

Golfer: If you laugh at me again, I'll knock your block off.
Caddy: You wouldn't even know what club to use.

• •

The two golfers were introduced on the first tee. Before starting off one tried to arrange some sort of a match.

"My handicap is 14. What's yours?" he asked his new companion.

"A bad back, lumbago, weak wrists and an incurable slice," came the ready response.

• •

A historian says that a game something like golf was played in 1089 A.D. This game is played still.

• •

Then there's the terrible temper type of golfer who says he can't afford to break 80 . . . because golf clubs are too expensive these days.

• •

Then there's the story of the thoughtful wife. She died early in the week so her funeral wouldn't interfere with her husband's Saturday golf game.

• •

Caddy to player who asked for advice, "Your trouble is you stand too close to the ball . . . after you've hit it."

• •

One statistician says there are more than 320 kinds of games played with balls. We, personally, have seen more than 320 kinds of games played with golf balls.

• •

A golf professional, hired by a big department store to give golf lessons, was approached by two women.

"Do you wish to learn to play golf, madam?" he asked one.

"Oh, no," she said, "it's my friend who wants to learn. I learned yesterday."

IS THERE A DOCTOR IN THE HOUSE?

People who think time heals everything haven't tried sitting it out in a doctor's waiting room.

· ·

A specialist is a doctor who has trained his patients to become ill during office hours.

· ·

They say that one in every four Americans is unbalanced. Think of your three closest friends. If they seem OK, then you're in trouble.

· ·

Woman: Do I have Asiatic Flu?
Doctor: No, you have Egyptian flu.
Woman: What is that?
Doctor: You're going to become a mummy.

· ·

An acupuncture specialist, annoyed by a late-night call from a patient, told the man, "Take two pins and call me in the morning."

· ·

A patient was brought to a psychiatrist by his family. They explained that he was suffering delusions that a huge fortune was awaiting him. He was expecting two letters which would give him details on a diamond mine he would inherit in Africa and a rubber plantation in Sumatra. The doctor explained, "It was a tough case, I devoted many hours to the patient and just when I had him completely cured, the two letters came."

· ·

A pretty young girl had broken off her engagement with a young doctor.

"Do you mean to tell me," exclaimed her girl friend, "that he actually asked you to return all his presents?"

"Not only that," she replied. "He sent me a bill for thirty-five house calls."

•   •

An elderly gentleman wasn't feeling well, and became irritated with his doctor because he wasn't getting better after five visits.

"Look!" said the doctor. "I'm doing all I can to help you. I can't make you younger."

"I wasn't particularly interested in getting younger." said the old man. "I just want to continue growing older."

•   •

The psychiatrist said sternly to the patient: "If you think you're walking out of here cured after only three sessions, you're crazy."

•   •

Psychiatrist: Congratulations, sir, you're cured.
Patient: Some cure. Before I was Julius Caesar. Now I'm nobody.

•   •

Patient: Doctor, I wish you'd give me something to make me smarter.
Doctor: Take these pills and come back next week.
Patient: (a week later) Doctor, I don't think I'm getting any smarter.
Doctor: Take some more of those pills and come back next week.
Patient: (a week later) I know I'm not any smarter. Are these pills candy?
Doctor: Now you're getting smarter.

•   •

The doctor felt the patient's purse and decided there was no hope.

• •

Doctor: Ever had a serious illness?
Patient: No.
Doctor: Ever had an accident?
Patient: No.
Doctor: You mean you have never had a single accident in your life?
Patient: Never, except last spring when a bull tossed me over a fence.
Doctor: Well, don't you call that an accident?
Patient: No, sir! He did it on purpose.

• •

Patient: (Calling very late at night) I can't sleep, Doctor. Can you do anything for me?
Doctor: Hold the phone for a minute and I'll sing you a lullaby.

• •

A minor operation is one performed on somebody else.

• •

His ailment is not a chronic but a chronicle.

• •

A patient complained to a friend that although he talked and talked, his psychiatrist never said a word.

A week later he told his friend he had a new problem: the analyst had died.

"What's the difference?" asked the friend. "Keep going."

• •

Doctor: Why do you have V-37821 tattooed on your back?

Patient: That's not tattooed. That's where my wife ran into me while I was opening the garage door.

• •

Patient one: That man wasn't a painless dentist like he advertised.
Patient two: Why? Did he hurt you?
Patient one: No, but he yelled when I bit his thumb, just like any other dentist.

• •

Stranger: Good morning, doctor, I just dropped in to tell you how much I benefited from your treatment.
Doctor: But you're not one of my patients.
Stranger: I know. But my Uncle Bill was and I'm his heir.

• •

Every chair in the doctor's waiting room was filled and some patients were standing. At one point the conversation died down and there was silence. During the silence an old man stood up wearily and remarked: "Well, guess I'll go home and die a natural death."

• •

The latest thing in shock treatment is a psychiatrist who sends his bills in advance.

• •

I used to be terribly conceited, buy my psychiatrist straightened me out and now I'm one of the nicest guys in town.

• •

Patient: I want the truth, doctor. Am I going to get well?
Doctor: Why, of course you are. You're going to get well if it costs every cent you have.

LOVE AT FIRST SIGHT

The cure for love at first sight . . . second sight.

• •

Most fellows never come to life until their engines go dead.

• •

Little girl: (to bride at wedding reception) You don't look nearly as tired as I should have thought.
Bride: Don't I, dear? But why did you think I should look tired?
Little girl: Well, I heard Mom and Dad say that you'd been running after Mr. McKee for months and months.

• •

Love may be blind, but it seems to be able to find its way around in the dark.

• •

Bill: Am I the only man you ever have kissed?
Sue: Yes, and by far the best looking.

• •

College is the only vacation a boy gets between his mother and his wife.

• •

Girl: No! I can't give you another dance. But I'll introduce you to the prettiest girl in the room.
Boy: But I don't want to dance with the prettiest girl in the room. I want to dance with you!

• •

Joe: I don't get much of a kick out of kissing girls.
Moe: I never heard one complain either.

• •

Girl: I'm so glad we're engaged.
Boy: But you knew all the time that I love you, didn't you?
Girl: Yes, dear, I knew it, but you didn't.

• •

A young man wrote a note to his girl friend which said, "If you love me, wear a red rose in your corsage tonight at the play. If my devotion to you is hopeless, wear a white rose." She wore a yellow rose.

• •

Life is just one fool thing after another. Love is just two fool things after each other.

• •

A kiss is the shortest distance between two.

• •

He: I dreamed I was married to the most beautiful girl in the world.
She: Were we happy?

• •

Absence makes the heart go wander.

• •

Girl: And are mine the only lips you have kissed?
Boy: Yes, and they are the sweetest of all.

• •

Two young lovers were trying to find a spot to be alone in while they had a long embrace. They were unable to find a secluded area so they decided to go the railway station where they could pretend that they were kissing goodbye. A porter who watched them for a period of time came up and said, "Why don't you take her around to the bus terminal? They go every three minutes from there."

• •

A hopeful young lady listed her requirements with a computer dating service. She wanted someone who liked people, wasn't too tall, preferred formal attire and enjoyed water sports. The computer followed her wishes exactly: it sent her a penguin.

•　•

A bachelor is a selfish, callous, undeserving man who has cheated some worthy woman out of a divorce.

•　•

When Cupid hits the mark he usually Mrs. it.

•　•

Stealing a kiss may be petty larceny, but sometimes its grand.

•　•

She: If I refuse to be your wife, will you really commit suicide?
He: That has been my usual procedure.

•　•

He: I promise you, the next time you contradict me, I'm going to kiss you.
She: Oh, no, you're not!

•　•

Never let a fool kiss you and never let a kiss fool you.

•　•

Bill: How much will a marriage license cost me?
Mark: Three dollars down, and your income for life.

•　•

Boy: Sweetheart, if I'd known that tunnel was so long, I'd have given you a kiss.
Girl: Gracious! Wasn't that you?

•　•

Mike: What do you call a man who's been lucky in love?
Joe: A bachelor.

●　　●

Love is sometimes like a poisoned mushroom. You can't tell if it's the real thing until it's too late.

●　　●

Girl: Whenever I look at you, I'm reminded of a famous man.
Boy: You flatter me. Who was the man?
Girl: Darwin.

●　　●

Her: I suppose all geniuses are conceited.
Him: Some of them . . . but I'm not.

●　　●

He: I know I'm not really much to look at.
She: Oh, well, you'll be at the office most of the time.

●　　●

Boy: If you refuse to be mine, I'll hurl myself off that five hundred foot cliff over there.
Girl: That's a lot of bluff.

●　　●

Mary: Well, what happened when you showed the girls in the office your new engagement ring? Did they all admire it?
Sara: Better than that, four of them recognized it.

●　　●

He: They say kisses are the language of love.
She: Well, why don't you say something?

●　　●

GOSSIP

A flying rumor never has any trouble in making a landing.

• •

Hear no evil, see no evil, speak no evil, and you'll never be a success at a tea party.

• •

Gossip, unlike river water, flows both ways.

• •

If nobody knows the trouble you've seen, you don't live in a small town.

• •

A closed mouth gathers no foot.

• •

The most knocking seems to be done by those who aren't able to ring the bell.

• •

Maybe dog is man's best friend because he wags his tail instead of his tongue.

• •

When you are in deep water, it's a good idea to keep your mouth shut.

• •

It takes two to speak truth . . . . one to speak and another to hear.

• •

We are advised to turn a deaf ear to every form of scandal and gossip . . . but not many of us have deaf ears.

• •

It's easy for folks to make monkeys of themselves just by carrying tales.

• •

It seems a shame to repeat gossip, but what else can you do with it?

FAMILY FOOLISHNESS

"Your son is making good progress on the piano. He is beginning to play quite nice tunes."

"Do you really think so? We were afraid that we'd merely gotten used to it."

• •

I've never been able to understand why women's hats are all different. I guess it's because no one wants to make the same mistake twice.

• •

When company stays too long, just treat them like members of the family and they'll soon leave.

• •

Father: Did Paul bring you home last night?
Daughter: Yes, it was late, Daddy. Did the noise disturb you?
Father: No, my dear, it wasn't the noise. It was the silence.

• •

A mother of twelve was asked how in the world she could take care of all her children.

"Well," she replied. "When I only had one it took all my time . . . so how could eleven more make any difference?"

• •

Friend: So your son is in college . . . what's he going to be when he gets through?
Father: Senile.

• •

"This is an ideal spot for a picnic."
   "It must be. Fifty million insects can't be wrong."

• •

We are told that healthy babies should be a delicate pink. Most are robust yellers.

• •

Son: Dad, does bigamy mean that a man has one wife too many?
Dad: Not necessarily, son. A man can have one wife too many and still not be a bigamist.

• •

My teenage daughter is at the stage where she's all skin and phones.

• •

Sister: I think there's company downstairs.
Brother: How d'ya know?
Sister: I just heard Mama laugh at Papa's joke.

• •

The person who invented summer camps ought to get the Nobel Peace Prize.

• •

I've wanted to run away from home more often since I've had kids than when I was a boy.

• •

Youngster, as Dad reads bedtime story: "Mommy, he's speed-reading again."

• •

36

Billy: Can I have a chocolate-chip cooky?
Mother: How do you ask?
Billy: May I have a chocolate-chip cooky?
Mother: What do you say?
Billy: May I please have a chocolate-chip cooky?
Mother: No, it's too close to supper.

•   •

Wife, to husband: "George, you had better help Johnny with his homework now, while you can. Next year he goes to the fourth grade."

•   •

Your conscience is the thing that makes you tell your mother before your sister does.

•   •

Bride's father to groom: "My boy, you're the second happiest man in all the world."

•   •

The proud father brought home a backyard swing set for his children and immediately started to assemble it with all the neighborhood children anxiously waiting to play on it. After several hours of reading the directions, attempting to fit bolt A into slot B, etc., he finally gave up and called upon an old handyman working in the neighboring yard.

The old timer came over, threw the directions away, and in a short while had the set completely assembled.

"It's beyond me," said the father, "how you got it together without even reading the instructions."

"To tell you the truth," replied the old-timer, "I can't read . . . and when you can't read, you've got to think."

•   •

The father of a couple of teenagers called the telephone company and announced: "I want to report an obscene phone bill."

• •

These trash compactors are nothing new. We've had one for years . . . it's called a closet.

• •

Every adult needs a child to teach; it's the way adults learn.

• •

Every young man should learn to take criticism. He'll probably be a parent someday.

• •

Father: I want you home by 11 p.m.
Daughter: But Father, I'm no longer a child.
Father: I know, that's why I want you home by 11.

• •

There are three stages in a man's life:
1. My daddy can whip your daddy.
2. Ah, Dad, you don't know anything.
3. My father used to say . . . .

• •

Wife: I'm happy to see that the neighbors finally returned our lawn mower before they moved. They certainly had it long enough.
Husband: OUR lawn mower? I just bought it at the garage sale they're having.

• •

Neighbor: I understand your son is on the football team. What position does he play?
Father: I think he's one of the drawbacks.

• •

The quickest way for a parent to get a child's attention is to sit down and look comfortable.

• •

Here's my report card . . . and I'm tired of watching TV anyway."

• •

A little girl, being punished by her mother, went to her desk and wrote on a piece of paper. Then going out in the yard she dug a hole in the ground, put the paper in it, and covered it over. The mother was interested, and when her child had gone away she dug up the paper and read: "Dear Devil: Please come and take my mamma away."

• •

Mother: Hush! You two children are always quarreling. Why can't you agree once in a while?
Son: We do agree, Mamma. Joan wants the largest piece of cake and so do I.

• •

The kind lady stopped to tell the sobbing little girl not to cry, and she offered as a convincing argument:
"You know it makes little girls homely."
The child stared at the benevolent lady, and then remarked:
"You must have cried an awful lot when you was young."

• •

A mother rebuked her daughter and put her to bed for being cross and ill tempered throughout the day. After she had been neatly tucked in the little one commented:
"It's temper when it's me an' nerves when it's you."

• •

"Dad."

"Yes, son."

"It says here, 'A man is known by the company he keeps.' Is that so?"

"Yes, son."

"Well, if a good man keeps company with a bad man, is the good man bad because he keeps company with the bad man, or is the bad man good because he keeps company with the good man?"

• •

Aunt: Will you let me kiss you if I give you a penny?

Nephew: A penny! Why, I get more than that for taking medicine.

• •

When Billy came home from school, his mother asked him how he had made out in the essay contest sponsored by the fourth grade.

"Well, I didn't win a prize," he said, "but I did get a horrible mention."

• •

A small boy was sitting on his father's knee watching his mother as she painfully went through the very delicate operation of doing her hair in that most becoming wave effect.

"No waves for you, pa," said the infant philosopher, as he fondly polished his parent's bald head, "You,re all beach."

• •

Little Sue was sitting with her mother in church during the wedding of her older sister. Halfway through the service, she saw her mother crying.

"Why are you crying, Mama?" she asked. "It's not your wedding."

• •

The best way to keep teenagers at home is to create a happy environment . . . and let the air out of their tires.

• •

The secret of being a good parent is being able to put your foot down without putting it in your mouth.

• •

Getting the baby to sleep is the hardest when she is about eighteen years old.

• •

"To tell the truth, Doctor," said a hard-working housewife, "I've always wanted to have a nervous breakdown. But every time I was about to get around to it, it was time to fix somebody a meal."

• •

Before I got married I had six theories about bringing up children. Now I have six children . . . and no theories.

• •

One young mother, on receiving a nursery school report that described her daughter as "emotionally immature," asked with good sense, "If you can't be immature at three, when can you be?"

• •

"My son is really growing up. Only last week he was able to go to the psychiatrist all by himself."

• •

Mother: A telegrame from Harvey, dear.
Father: Well, did he pass the examination this time?
Mother: No, but he is almost at the top of the list of those who failed.

• •

The reason children are so happy is, they don't have any children of their own to worry about.

• •

"Excuse me for bothering you coming to the door for your daughter," apologized the young man, "but my horn isn't working."

• •

Husband: Now, look, Lucy. I don't want to seem harsh, but your mother has been living with us for twenty years now. Don't you think it's about time she got a place of her own?
Wife: MY mother? I thought she was your mother!

• •

Science has found that insanity is hereditary . . . parents get it from their children.

OPTIMISTS AND PESSIMISTS

An optimist is a man who thinks the time will come when there will be no more wisecrack definitions of an optimist.

• •

A pessimist is an optimist who endeavored to practice what he preached.

• •

Always borrow from a pessimist....he never expects it back anyhow.

• •

A 100 per cent optimist is a man who believes the thinning out of his hair is only a temporary matter.

• •

A Pessimist's version: Love cankers all.

• •

An optimist is a guy who tells you to cheer up when things are going his way.

• •

An optimist and a pessimist went into business together. Trade Flourished.
"Well," said the optimist, "we've had a wonderful month. It's been one constant run of customers."
Yeah," agreed the pessimist, "we have had some good business. But look at those front doors! If people keep shoving through them, the hinges will be worn out in another week."

• •

Optimistic Bachelor: Let's get married!
Pessimistic Spinster: Good Heavens! Who'd have us?

• •

The most optimistic person I ever met was undoubtedly a young man who went into a seafood restaurant and ate a dozen oysters in the hope of finding a pearl to pay the bill.

• •

The king pin optimist of the world is the man who thinks he can teach his wife how to drive an automobile.

• •

A pessimist remembers the lily belongs to the onion family, an optimist that the onion belongs to the lily family.

• •

The optimist fell from the top story of a skyscraper. As he passed the tenth story, he was overheard muttering:
"So far, so good!"

• •

POLITICS

Governmental machinery is the marvelous device which enables ten men to do the work of one.

• •

A political leader was trying to clarify his response to a reporter's question. "To the best of my knowledge," he said, "I'm not sure."

• •

Did you hear about the new Politician Dance?....two steps forward, one step backward, then sidestep.

• •

The cheapest way to have your family tree traced is to run for a public office.

• •

The love of money is also the root of all congressional investigations.

• •

The Southern father was introducing his family of boys to a visiting govenor.
"Thirteen boys," exclaimed the Govenor. "And all Democrats, I suppose."
"All but one," said the father proudly. "They're all Democrats but Willie, the little rascal. He got to readin'."

• •

A prominent Republican Party leader was explaining how he secured votes for the party. I always give every cab driver a healthy tip and then tell him, "Vote Republican."
"I use about the same method," said a Democrat opponent. "Only it's a lot cheaper. I don't give them any tip and tell them to vote Republican."

• •

Two political candidates were having a hot debate. Finally one of them jumped up and yelled at the other: "What about the powerful interests that control you?"

And the other guy screamed back: "You leave my wife out of this."

. .

The political bee that buzzes in many a bonnet is a hum-bug.

. .

The politician is my shepherd....I am in want;
He maketh me to lie down on park benches,
He leadeth me beside the still factories;
He disturbeth my soul,
Yea, though I walk through the valley of the shadow of depression and recession,
I anticipate no recovery, for he is with me.
He prepareth a reduction in my salary in the presence of my enemies;
He anointeth my small income with great losses;
My expenses runneth over.
Surely unemployment and poverty shall follow me all the days of my life.
And I shall dwell in a mortagaged house forever.

. .

GOOD NEWS AND BAD NEWS

Good news: You've made the Olympic javelin team.
Bad news: Your job is to catch the javelin.

. .

Bad news: Your wife just ran off with your best friend.
Good news: That's two people off your Christmas list.

. .

Bad news: The crops have failed and we have nothing to eat but lizards.
Good news: There aren't enough to go around.

• •

Good news: Mr. Columbus, land is only twenty miles away.
Bad news: According to our calculations, it's straight down.

• •

Good news: You've won the State lottery and a total of one million dollars.
Bad news: My name is Smith and I'm with the Internal Revenue Service.

• •

Bad news: We have a hijacker aboard the plane.
Good news: He wants to go to the French Riviera.

• •

Bad news: We seem to have lost your luggage.
Good news: There'll be no charge for the 60 pounds overweight.

• •

Good news: Your son just broke the World's Record for High Diving.
Bad news: There was no water in the pool

• •

Good news: In this test tube I have all the male chromosomes....and in this jar I have all the female chromosomes....when I pour the test tube into the jar, I will create life.
Bad news: We can't do it tonight because the jar has a headache.

• •

Bad news: We removed the wrong lung.
Good news: The other lung is coming along fine.

• •

Good news: All of you slaves on the galley are going to get a extra special ration of rum with the noon meal.
Bad news: After lunch, the captain wants to go water skiing.

• •

Bad news: Your new sports car just drove off the ridge into the Grand Canyon.
Good news: It got 49 miles to the gallon on the way down.

• •

Bad news: Your wife was captured by cannibals.
Worse news: They have already eaten.

RETALIATION

Wife: Such an odd thing happened today. The clock fell off the wall, and if it had fallen a moment sooner, it would have hit mother.
Husband: I always said that clock was slow.

• •

Artist: I'd like to devote my last picture to some charitable purpose.
Critic: Why not give it to an institution for the blind?

• •

Husband: Ouch! I bumped my crazy bone.
Wife: Oh, well, comb your hair right and the bump won't show.

• •

First man: I wonder if that fat old girl is really trying to flirt with me?

Second man: I can easily find out by asking her....she is my wife.

• •

I wouldn't call him a liar. Let's just say he lives on the wrong side of the facts.

• •

A car screeched to a halt at an intersection, barely missing an elder lady. But instead of giving him the tounge lashing he deserved, she smiled sweetly, and pointed to a pair of baby shoes dangling from his rear view mirror.

"Young man," she said, "you really shouldn't drive without your shoes on."

• •

The president of the local Women's Club was telling her husband of their plans to raise money for the club.

"We're going to serve as Caddies-for-a-Day at the Country Club, but don't know what to call ourselves. We've thought of Caddie-etts and Links Lassies, but we need something more original."

"I have it," offered her husband. "How about Tee-Bags?"

• •

The young lady eyed her escort with great disapproval. "That's the fourth time you've gone back for more ice cream and cake, Wilbert," she said acidly. "Doesn't it embarrass you at all?"

"Why should it?" the hungry fellow shrugged. "I keep telling them I'm getting it for you."

• •

I don't recall your face but your breath is familiar!

• •

The reason ideas die quickly in some people's heads is because they can't stand solitary confinement.

• •

There are still a lot of wide open spaces left in this country. The only trouble is most of them are surrounded by teeth.

• •

A bore is someone who goes on talking while you're interrupting.

• •

Joe: Do you believe in the Darwinian theory?
Moe: Yes. In fact, I go even farther than Darwin did. I believe that some members of our species have started on the return journey.

• •

Two women in a train argued concerning the window at last one called the conductor.
"If this window is open," she declared, "I shall catch a cold and die."
"If the window is shut," declared the other, "I shall suffocate."
The two glared at each other.
The conductor was at a loss, and welcomed the advice of a man who sat near. "First open the window," said the man, "That will kill one. Then shut the window; that will kill the other. Then we'll have peace."

• •

Bill: I've got a splinter in my finger.
Jill: How did you get it....scratch your head?

• •

A city man passed a boy husking corn and remarked, "Your corn looks yellow."

"That's the kind pa planted," said the boy.

"Looks as though you wouldn't get over half a crop," said the man.

"We won't," said the boy; "the landlord gets the other half."

"You're pretty near a fool, aren't you?" said the man.

"Yep, within ten feet of one."

• •

"His versatility is something extraordinary."

"I had an idea he was rather stupid."

"That's just it. I never met a man who could make more different kinds of a fool of himself."

• •

Actor: How do I rank as an actor?

Critic: You don't....you are.

• •

"You have a pretty place here, Bill," remarked the guest on the morning of his departure. "But it looks a bit bare yet."

"Oh, that's because the trees are so young," answered the host comfortably. "I hope they'll have grown to a good size before you come again."

• •

Husband: I hear that fish is brain food.

Wife: You had better eat a whale.

• •

Wife: You know the old saying, 'What you don't know won't hurt you?'

Husband: What about it?

Wife: You must really be safe.

• •

Caller: I know it's two o'clock in the morning....I do hope I haven't disturbed you.
Man: Oh, no, that's quite all right. I had to get up to answer the telephone anyway.

• •

Two people were discussing a fat friend: "He's too big in the first place....and in the second place, too."

• •

A portly man was trying to get to his seat at the circus. "Pardon me," he said to a woman, "did I step on your foot?"
"Possibly so," she said, after glancing at the ring. "All the elephants are still out there. You must have."

• •

"Hey, you just gave me a nasty look!"
"You have a nasty look, all right, but I didn't give it to you."

• •

A man who was invited to a house party he didn't wish to attend, telegraphed to the hostess: "Regret I can't come. Complete lie follows by letter."

• •

He is the type of person who keeps the conversation ho-humming.

• •

Social tact is making your company feel at home, even though you wish they were.

• •

"He's not as big as a fool as he used to be."
"Getting wiser?"
"No, thinner."

• •

He: She certainly is polished, don't you think so?
She: Yeah. Everything she says cast a reflection on someone.

• •

If the principal function of dressing is to cover weaknesses, I suggest that you wear a hat.

• •

The customer settled himself and let the barber put the towel around him. Then he told the barber, "Before we start, I know the weather's awful. I don't care who wins the next big fight, and I don't bet on the horse races. I know I'm getting thin on top, but I don't mind. Now get on with it!"

"Well, sir, if you don't mind," said the barber, "I'll be able to concentrate better if you don't talk so much!"

• •

Mr. Highbrow: I wonder why the magician wanted to borrow my new mink coat?
Mrs. Lowbrow: He probably wanted to pull rabbits out of it.

• •

Smith: I heard the word 'Idiot.' Are you referring to me?
Jones: Don't be so conceited. There are other idiots in the world!

• •

LAW AND ORDER

Judge: Give your name, occupation, and the charge against you.
Prisoner: My name is Spark, I'm an electrician, and the charge is battery.
Judge: Alright, officer, put him in a dry cell.
Prisoner: This is a terrible shock.

• •

"What is your occupation?" asked the judge sternly. "I haven't any," replied the man. "I just circulate around, so to speak."
"Please note," said the judge turning to the clerk, "that this gentleman is retired from circulation for thirty days."

• •

Judge: Did you steal this man's television set?
Thief: Oh, I only took it for a joke.
Judge: How far did you carry it?
Thief: From his house to mine....about three miles.
Judge: Six months in jail. That was carrying a joke too far.

• •

A burglar, needing money to pay his income taxes, decided to burgle the safe in a store. On the safe door he was much pleased to find a note reading: "Please don't use dynamite. This safe is not locked. Just turn the knob." He did so. Instantly a heavy sandbag fell on him, the entire premises were flood-lighted, and alarm bells started clanging. As the police carried him out on a stretcher, he was heard moaning: "My confidence in human nature has been rudely shaken."

• •

We pay a tremendous crime bill each year....but we do get a lot of crime for our money.

•   •

Two drivers were surveying the damage to their cars following an accident. One pulled out a bottle and offered the other a drink saying: "It'll help calm you down."
"Thanks," replied the other, taking a swig and returning the bottle. "Aren't you having one, too?"
"Yes," said the other, "but I think I'll wait until after the cops have been here and gone."

•   •

A small boy was trying to explain a broken window to a policeman: "I was cleaning my slingshot and it went off."

•   •

Judge: All you say goes in at one ear and out at the other.
Lawyer: What is to prevent it?

•   •

A juryman petitioned the court to be excused, declaring: "I owe a man fifty dollars that I borrowed, and as he is leaving town to-day for some years I want to catch him before he gets to the plane and pay him the money."
"You are excused," the judge announced in a very cold voice. "I don't want anybody on the jury who can lie like you."

•   •

A traffic policeman hailed down a speeding automobile.
"You were going 90 in a fifty-five mile per hour zone," said the policeman.

"So, what," came the reply. "It's a free country, isn't it?"

"Let's see your driver's license," said the policeman.

"Never had one, I can drive just as well without it."

"You also have last year's plates on your car," said the policeman. "That's three charges against you."

At this point the driver's wife spoke up and said, "Never mind him, officer. He always talks this way when he's drunk."

•   •

Judge: You say you want a divorce because your husband is careless about his appearance?

Wife: That's right, judge. He hasn't shown up in almost two years.

•   •

"Pull over to the curb," said the policeman. "You don't have a taillight."

The motorist stepped out, looked in back of the car and stood quivering and speechless. "Oh, it's not that bad," said the policeman.

The man mumbled, "It's not the taillight I'm worried about....where is my wife and trailer?"

•   •

The district attorney was cross examining the murderess.

"And after you had poisoned the coffee and your husband sat at the breakfast table partaking of the fatal dosage, didn't you feel any qualms? Didn't you feel the slightest pity for him knowing he was about to die and was wholly unaware of it?"

"Yes, there was a moment when I sort of felt sorry for him."

"When was that?"

"When he asked for the second cup."

•   •

A young attorney had been talking for about four hours to a jury, who, when he had finished, felt like lynching him.

His opponent, a grizzled old professional, then arose and, looking sweetly at the judge said, "Your honor, I will follow the example of my young friend who has just finished and submit the case without argument."

• •

The witness was a proud lady who had lost the bloom of youth quite some time ago. The young lawyer thinking it would be to his advantage to get her rattled said: "And now, madam, I must ask you a rather personal question. How old are you?"

"Young man," she replied, "the judge just instructged you that we could have no hearsay evidence, and I don't remember being born. All my knowledge is hearsay."

• •

Robber: This is a holdup! Give me your money or else.
Man: Or else what?
Robber: Don't confuse me, this is my first job.

• •

The sharp young attorney was cross examining an elderly witness to an accident.

"You say you were about 40 feet from the scene of the accident? Let me remind you that you're 86 years old. Just how far can you see clearly?

The old man responded, "Well, when I wake up I see the sun and they tell me that's about 93 million miles away."

• •

The woman called to the stand was handsome but no longer young. The judge gallantly instructed, "Let the witness state her age, after which she may be sworn.

•   •

"Will you tell the court how far you were from the spot where the shooting occurred?" asked the defense counsel.
"I was exactly fourteen feet, three and one-half inches," replied the witness.
"How can you be sure of the exact distance?" asked the lawyer.
"I measured it because I was sure sooner or later some fool would ask that question."

•   •

Judge: And how do you plead?
Man: I plead guilty and waive the hearing
Judge: What do you mean, 'Waive the hearing?'
Man: I mean I don't want to hear no more about it.

•   •

A judge sat on the bench for a long, long time, while a lawyer addressed the court endlessly. Finally the judge dispatched a note to the lawyer. It read:

PATIENCE COMPETITION

GOLD MEDAL....ME

HONORABLE MENTION....JOB.

The lawyer wound up in a hurry.

•   •

"What profession is your boy going to select?"
"I'm going to educate him to be a lawyer. He's naturally argumentative and bent on mixing into other people's troubles and he might just as well as get paid for his time."

•   •

The burglars had tied and gagged the bank cashier after extracting the combination to the safe and had herded the other employees into a separate room under guard. After they rifled the safe and were about to leave, the cashier made desperate pleading noises through the gag. Moved by curiosity one of the burglars loosened the gag.

"Please!" whispered the cashier, "Take the books, too....I'm $8,500 short."

•　•

"Repeat the words the defendant used," said the lawyer.

"I'd rather not. They were not fit words to tell a gentleman."

"Then, whisper them to the judge."

•　•

In Colorado a mining claim was pending before a judge with a reputation for a free and easy brand of justice. One morning His Honor remarked:

"Gentlemen, this court has in hand a check from the plaintiff in this case for $10,000 and a check from the defendant for $15,000. The court will return $5,000 to the defendant. Then we will try the case strictly on its merits."

•　•

Judge: You are charged with throwing your mother-law out of the window.

Man: I done it without thinking, sir.

Judge: Yes, but don't you see how dangerous it might have been for anyone passing at the time?

SUNDAY FUNNIES

On Church sign: COME EARLY....IF YOU WANT A BACK SEAT.

• •

A evangelist was speaking in a meeting when a heckler shouted, "Listen to him! And his father used to drive a wagon led by a donkey."
"That's right," said the evangelist, "and today my father and the wagon are gone. But I see we still have the donkey with us."

• •

Church member: Pastor, you have a marvelous gift of oratory. How did you develop it?
Pastor: I learned to speak as men learn to skate or ride a bike....by doggedly making a fool of myself until I got used to it.

• •

Ministers fall into four categories:
1. Those who do not have any notes and the people have no idea how long he will speak.
2. Those who put down on the podium in front of them each page of their sermon as they read it. These honest ones enable the audience to keep track of how much more is to come.
3. Those who cheat by putting each sheet of notes under the others in their hand.
4. And, worst of all, those who put down each sheet of notes as they read them and then horrify the audience by picking up the whole batch and reading off the other side.

• •

The Devil's traps are never set in the middle of God's road.

• •

Teacher: What parable in the Bible do you like best?
Student: The one about the fellow that loafs and fishes.

• •

Father: And what did you learn in Sunday School this morning?
Son: That I am a child of Satan.

• •

Sermons are like babies....easy to conceive....hard to deliver.

• •

Teacher: Who were the twin boys in the Bible?
Student: That's easy, First and Second Samuel.

• •

The retiring usher was instructing his youthful successor in the details of his office. "And remember, my boy, that we have nothing but good, kind Christians in this church....until you try to put someone else in their pew."

• •

I spoke in one church that was so small that when I took a bow I hit my head on the back pew.

• •

Pastor: Just think of it, Jonah spent three days in the belly of a large fish.
Member: That's nothing, my husband spent longer than that in the belly of an alligator.
Pastor: Well, I declare....just how long was he in there?
Member: It's almost four years, now.

• •

At a Sunday school picnic the minister, while walking across a small footbridge, was seized with a fit of sneezing. His false teeth flew from his mouth and landed in the clear water in the middle of the stream. Much worried and embarrassed, the minister was preparing to remove his shoes and wade in after them when a dear little gray-haired grandmother appeared on the scene, carrying a well-filled dinner basket. When she discovered the minister's plight, she reached in her basket, removed a crisp, brown chicken leg, tried a string to it and tossed it into the water near the dentures. Quickly the teeth clamped into the chicken leg and were hauled to safety.

• •

On Church sign: COME IN AND HAVE YOUR FAITH LIFTED.

• •

One reason we have so many pennies in the church collection plate is because we have no smaller coin.

• •

A minister was speaking to a class of boys on the merits of moral courage. "Ten boys were sleeping in a dormitory," said he by way of illustration, "and only one knelt down to say his prayers. That is moral courage."

When he had finished his talk he asked one boy to give him an example of moral courage.

"Please, sir," said the lad, "ten ministers were sleeping in a dormitory and only one jumped into bed without saying his prayers."

• •

Member: How did you like the minister's sermon?
Friend: Well, frankly, I like our own minister better.
Member: Why is that?
Friend: It's the words they use. Our minister says, "In conclusion," and then he concludes. Your minister says, "Lastly," and he lasts.

• •

The preacher of a small church in a remote section of the country once preached a funeral service of one of the local mountaineers and he explained the deceased's position in the community thusly:

"Now, he wasn't what you call a good man, because he never gave his heart to the Lord; but he was what you'd call a respected sinner."

• •

Three fellows went to church and when it came time to pass the plate, the three discovered they had no money. Not wanting to be embarrassed, one fainted and the other two carried him out.

• •

"What is a prime minister?"
"A prime minister is a preacher at his best."

• •

A three-year-old version of the 23rd Psalm: "....He leadeth me beside distilled water."

• •

A village pastor, who had a weakness for trout, preached against fishing on Sunday. The next day one of his members presented him with a fine string of fish and said, hesitatingly: "I guess I ought to tell you, parson, that those trout were caught on Sunday." The minister gazed appreciatively at the speckled trout, and said piously, "The fish aren't to blame for that."

• •

Teacher: Johnny, you shouldn't talk so loudly in Sunday School.
Johnny: Billy Graham does.

• •

Little Timmy was saying his prayers one night. His

mother overheard this entreaty: "And please make Tommy stop throwing things at me. By the way, I've mentioned this before."

•   •

A visitor to a drought-stricken area was engaged in conversation at the local store about the "no-rain" situation.
"You think the drought is bad here," the merchant observed, "But down south o' here a ways, they haven't had any for so long that the Baptists are sprinkling, the Methodists are using a damp cloth, and the Presbyterians are issuing rain checks!"

•   •

"Always remember we are here to help others," said a mother as she explained the Golden Rule.
Her little one meditated for a moment and inquired, "Well, what are the others here for?"

•   •

Teacher: Today I shall tell you a Bible story on Moses and the plagues sent on the people of Egypt. Does anyone know what a plague is?
Student: Yes, my brother is one.

•   •

Teacher: Who was sorry when the prodigal son returned home?
Student: The fatted calf.

•   •

Teacher: Why was Solomon the wisest man in the world?
Student: Because he had so many wives to advise him.

•   •

Deacon: It says here, "The wicked flee when no man pursueth."

Pastor: Yes, that is true, but they make much better time when somebody is after them.

• •

Billy: What are prayers anyway?

Mother: They are messages sent to Heaven.

Billy: Well....do I pray at night because the rates are cheaper?

• •

Teacher: Why did Jesus know the Scriptures so well?

Student: Oh, that's easy. His Daddy wrote them.

• •

The pastor visited the Sunday evening youth group and volunteers were called on to pray. A little girl volunteered to pray for the pastor. Her prayer: "Be with our pastor and help him to preach a better sermon next Sunday."

• •

A minister told his congregation that there were 739 different sins. He already has received 73 requests for the list.

• •

Five-year-old Johnny was being urged by his mother to take some medicine.

"It's good for you, Johnny. And God wishes you to take it."

"I don't believe He does, Mother. I'll ask him." The youngster buried his head under the blankets on his bed and soon a hoarse voice came, "No, certainly not!"

• •

A minister who paid more attention to the pleasures of life than to his sermons was taken to task for his worldliness by his Quaker friend. The rebuke he received was tactful. "Friend," said the Quaker, "I understand thee's clever at fox-catching."

"I have few equals and no superiors at that sport," the minister replied complacently.

"Nevertheless, friend," said the Quaker, "if I were a fox I would hide where thee never would find me."

"Where would you hide?" asked the minister with a frown.

"Friend, I would hide in thy study."

• •

Men do not usually reject the Bible because it contradicts itself, but because it contradicts them.

• •

Pastor: What do we learn from the story of Eutychus, the young man who, listening to the preaching of the Apostle Paul, fell asleep and, falling out of a window, was taken up dead?

Member: Ministers should learn not to preach too long sermons.

• •

Well, what are you sneering about? You don't seem to have much faith in my good resolutions."

"I was just wondering if you had taken the paving contract for the next world."

• •

Two Chinamen were heard discussing the denominational difference between the Baptists, Methodists and English Friends. One of them said to the other:

"They say these denominations have different beliefs. Just what is the difference between them?"

"Oh," said the other, "not much! Big washee, little washee, and no washee, that is all.

• •

Agnostic: If those Christians would stop building such large and fancy buildings and give the money to the poor it would be more to their credit.
Christian: I've heard that remark before.
Agnostic: Indeed! And by who, may I ask?
Christian: Judas Iscariot.

• •

Two little girls had a violent tussle with each other and the mother of one of them said in reprimand to her daughter:

"It was Satan who suggested to you to pull Jenny's hair."

"I shouldn't be surprised," said the little girl. "But kicking her in the shins was entirely my own idea."

• •

"Does your husband attend church regularly?"

"Oh, yes. He hasn't missed an Easter Sunday since we were married."

• •

A pastor always used the phrase, "It might be worse." when some calamity would come his way. One day a friend said to him, "I've something to tell you, and you won't be able to use your favorite phrase. I dreamt last night that I died and went to hell." "It might be worse," said the preacher. "Man alive, how could it be worse?" "It might be true."

• •

The little girl reported at home what she had learned at Sunday School concerning the creation of Adam and Eve:

"The teacher told us how God made the first man and the first woman. He made the man first. But the man was very lonely with nobody to talk to him. So God put the man to sleep. And while the man was asleep, God took out his brains and made a woman of them."

•   •

Some go to church to weep, while others go to sleep.
Some go to tell their woes, others to show their clothes.
Some go to hear the preacher, others like the solo screecher.
Boys go to reconnoiter, girls go because they orter.
Many go for good reflections, precious few to help collections.

•   •

When it comes to giving, some people stop at nothing.

•   •

After a family disturbance one of the little boys closed his bedtime prayer by saying, "And please don't give my dad any more children....He don't know how to treat those he's got now."

•   •

Three Kinds of Christians:
1. Rowboat Christians....
have to be pushed wherever they go.
2. Sailboat Christians....
always go with the wind.
3. Steam boat Christians....
make up their mind where they ought to go, and go there regardless of wind or weather.

•   •

Adam may have had his troubles, but at least he didn't have to listen to Eve talking about the man she could have married.

•   •

When the family returned from Sunday morning service father criticized the sermon, daughter thought the choir's singing was off key, and mother found fault with the organist's playing. The subject had to be dropped when the small boy of the family said, "But it was a good show for a nickel, don't you think, Dad?"

• •

A circuit preacher rode into a backwoods town and set up a series of camp meetings. The first evening he asked for a volunteer piano player so the congregation could sing. He promptly got a volunteer and the hymnals were distributed.

"All right," said the preacher. "Let's all sing hymn number 4."

"Sorry, preacher," said the piano player. "I don't know humn number four."

"That's O.K.," said the enthusiastic preacher. "We'll just sing hymn number twenty-seven. Everybody knows it."

The piano player squirmed a bit on his bench and said, "Sorry preacher, I don't know hymn number 27."

The preacher, keeping his good nature said, "Don't feel badly about it. We'll just sing hymn number 34. Everybody learned that when they were small children."

The piano player was really nervous by now and said, "Sorry preacher, but I guess I don't know hymn number 34.

Whereupon someone in the back shouted, "That piano player is an idiot!"

"Hold it!" exclaimed the preacher. "I want that man who called the piano player an idiot to stand up."

No one stood.

"If he won't stand up, I want the man sitting beside

the man who called the piano player an idiot to stand up."

No one stood.

After a brief period of complete silence, a little fellow in the back stood up and said, "Preacher, I didn't call the piano player an idiot, and I'm not sitting beside the man who called the piano player an idiot....what I want to know, is who called that idiot a piano player?"

• •

A collector of rare books ran into an acquaintance of his who had just thrown away an old Bible that had been in his family for generations. He happened to mention that Guten . . . something had printed it.

"Not Gutenberg?" gasped the book collector.

"Yes, that was the name."

"You idiot! You've thrown away one of the first books ever printed. A copy recently sold at auction for $400,000."

"Mine wouldn't have been worth a dime," replied the man. "Some clown by the name of Martin Luther had scribbled all over it."

• •

Conversation between Adam and Eve must have been difficult at times because they had nobody to talk about.

• •

Teacher: In our lesson today we have talked about the burnt offerings offered in the Old Testament. Why don't we have burnt offerings today.

Student: On account of air pollution.

• •

If God were permissive, He would have called them the Ten Suggestions.

VERY PUNNY

Walter: I've invented a new compass that always points the wrong way.
Frances: What do you call it?
Walter: I call it a Tates compass, because he who has a Tates is lost.

• •

There's another sad tale. This one is about the French-horn player whose toupee fell into his horn.... he spent the rest of the night blowing his top.

• •

Dave: My uncle can play the piano by ear.
Rich: That's nothing. My uncle fiddles with his whiskers.

• •

Successful acupuncture is a jab well done.

• •

Bob: I had my face lifted.
Esther: really, I don't see any difference.
Bob: It fell again when I saw the bill.

• •

The mosquito has no preference, he bites folks fat or thin.
But the welt that he raises, it itches like blazes.
And that's where "the rub" comes in.

• •

Two preachers were having lunch at a farm during the progress of certain anniversary celebrations. The farmer's wife cooked a couple of chickens, saying that the family could dine on the remains after the visitors had gone. But the hungry preachers wolfed the chickens bare.

Later the farmer was conducting his guests round the farm, when an old rooster commenced to crow ad lib. "Seems mighty proud of himself," said one of the guests.

"No wonder," growled the farmer, "he's got two sons in the ministry."

•   •

Once upon a time there lived a farmer who owned a big hayfield. The farmer's son decided to move to the city, and earn his living there. But when he got to the city the best he could do was a job as a bootblack at the railroad station. Now the farmer makes hay while the son shines.

•   •

Doctors claim that cheerful people resist diseases much better than glum ones. So remember, "The surly bird always catches the germ."

•   •

If you're traveling in Scandinavia and you come to the last Lapp, you must be near the Finnish line.

•   •

A man was walking down the street and noticed a sign reading, "Hans Schmidt's Chinese Laundry." Being of a curious nature he entered and was greeted by an obviously Oriental man who identified himself as Hans Schmidt.

"How come you have a name like that," inquired the stranger.

The Oriental explained in very broken English that when he landed in America he was standing in the immigration line behind a German. When asked his name the German replied, "Hans Schmidt." When the immigration official asked the Oriental his name he replied, "Sam Ting."

•   •

Once upon a time there was a witch who decided to open a tea-room. She picked a good location and at first she prospered. Then she decided to cut corners and make some real money.

The witch found that if she saved used teabags and used them over again, no one seemed to notice. Before long the greedy old witch was using the same tea-bags over and over and over again.

First her business dwindled. Then it faltered, and soon she was bankrupt.

Moral: Honest tea is the best policy.

• •

Before he died, the operator of a filtering plant willed his brain to science. The scientists were sorry to learn of his death, but happy to receive his brain. It was their first chance to examine a filtering man's thinker.

• •

Ken: Last night, by mistake, I drank a bottle of gold paint.
Melba: How do you feel this morning?
Ken: Guilty.

• •

Brad: I hear Cupid almost got you last week.
Chlarlie: Yes, I had an arrow escape.

• •

Rod: I represent the National Woolen Mills Institute. Could I interest you in some yarns?
Ron: Sure, go ahead. Let's hear a few."

• •

Incidentally, halitosis jokes are in bad odor so far as we are concerned.

• •

First Executioner: Is that so? Well last week I cut off more heads than you'll cut off in your whole life.

Second Executioner: Listen, bud, I've brought that old slicer down on the crowned heads of five countries.

Third Executioner: Come, come boys, let't not talk chop.

• •

Sharon: People say I have eyes like my father.

Bill: I get it....pop-eyed.

• •

"All right, you!" screamed the mother pigeon to her backward squab. "Either you learn to fly today or I'll tie a rope around you and tow you."

"Oh, mother, not that!" cried her baby. "I'd rather die than be pigeon-towed."

VISIT SMOGARIA

Jack: That' a queer pair of stockings you have on, Elmer....one is red and the other green.

Elmer: Yes, and I've got another pair like it at home.

• •

How would the Smogarians have fought the Viet Nam War? ....The same way we did!

• •

A bricklayer was laying bricks on the third story of a building and unfortunately dropped a brick on the head of a Smogarian who was mixing mortar down below.

The Smogarian yelled, "Hey! What do you think you are doing? You made me bite my tongue!"

• •

One good thing about being a Smogarian. You'll never miss an important phone call because you're in the bathtub.

• •

When a man complained in a Smogarian restaurant that he'd found a fly in his soup, the manager came running over and said, "Congratulations, all day long my waiters have been trying to catch that fly, and just imagine...you, a total stranger, have succeeded."

• •

Question: What is a Smogarian symphony orchestra?
Answer: Three kazoos and a radio.

• •

Song: Smogarian, Smogarian, Where does your garden grow?
Refrain: Usually under his fingernails.

• •

Question: Why are there so few Smogarian fashion models?
Answer: Because Smogarian girls drool instead of smile when the photographer says "Cheese!"

WEDLOCK OR DEADLOCK

A man is incomplete until he's married....then he's finished.

• •

Marriage is when a man gets hooked on his own line.

• •

Marriage is like a bath tub....once you are in it for awhile it's not so hot.

• •

There are two things that cause unhappy marriages ....men and women

• •

Keep your eyes open before marriage...half shut afterwards.

• •

Marriage is an institution. Marriage is love. Love is blind. Therefore marriage is an institution for the blind.

• •

About all that is necessary for a divorce nowadays is a wedding.

• •

This country will never adopt polygamy. The divorce courts couldn't stand the strain.

• •

They say brunetts have a sweeter disposition than blonds and redheads. Don't believe it! My wife has been all three and I couldn't see any difference.

• •

Marriage is like twirling a baton, turning handsprings, or eating with chopsticks....it looks so easy till you try it.

• •

Melba: My husband was named Man of the Year.
Pam: Well, that shows you what kind of a year it's been.

• •

Esther: Why did you get rid of your waterbed?
Sharon: Bill and I were drifting apart.

• •

Many a man has acquired a huge vocabulary by marrying it.

•   •

Every week it's the same pleasant routine. We arise, and my wife Pam prepares breakfast. As soon as she's finished, we get dressed and grab a bite at the restaurant.

•   •

Bufe: My wife has the worst memory I ever heard of.
Jay: Forgets everything, eh?
Bufe: No; remembers everything.

•   •

"I'll bet if I was married I'd be boss and tell my wife where to head in," declared the bachelor.
"Yes," retorted the old married man, "and I supose when you get to a railroad crossing you honk your horn to warn the oncoming train to get out of your way, don't you?"

•   •

Groom: How did you make this cake, dear?
Bride: Here's the recipe. I clipped it from a magazine.
Groom: Are you sure you read the right side? The other side tells how to make a rock garden.

•   •

Buck: This magazine article says that it takes the tusks of 4,700 elephants a year to make billiard balls.
Nancy: Isn't it wonderful that such big beasts can be taught to do such delicate work!

•   •

A man came home from work tired, but his eyes lighted up as he stepped inside his house and saw a beautiful layer cake with seven candles on it, on the dining room table. "A birthday cake! he exclaimed with pleasure. "Whose birthday is it?"

"Oh," replied his wife nonchalantly, "That's for the dress I've got on. It's seven years old today."

• •

The reason so few milkmen are married is that they see women too early in the morning.

• •

Wife to irate husband:"Normally I wouldn't dream of opening a letter addressed to you, but this one was marked "private."

• •

Jack: The lie detector is a marvelous invention. Have you ever seen one?
John: Seen one? I married one.

• •

Marriage teaches you loyalty, forbearance, self-restraint and a lot of other qualities you wouldn't need if you'd stayed single.

• •

A man appeared at a newspaper office to place an ad offering $1,000 reward for the return of his wife's pet cat.

"That's an awful price to pay for a cat," said the cler,.

"Not this one," replied the man. "I drowned it."

• •

Wife: My husband and I like the same things....but it took him 16 years to learn."

• •

Wife: You rat! Before we were married, you told me you were well off!
Husband: I was, but I didn't realize how well off.

• •

The angry wife called on her attorney and announced she wanted to sue her husband for divorce. "What grounds?" asked the attorney.

"Bigamy. I'll show him he can't have his Kate and Edith, too"

• •

Ken: I hear you advertised for a wife. Any replies?
Bob: Sure, hundreds.
Ken: What did they say?
Bob: They all said, "Here, take mine."

• •

Bill: I remember my wedding day very distinctly. I carried my new bride across the threshold of our little house and said, "Honey, this is your and my little world."
Bob: And I suppose you've lived happily ever after?
Bill: Well, not exactly. We've been fighting for the World's Championship ever since.

• •

"I came home, Your Honor, and found my wife in the arms of a strange man."
Judge: "And what did she say when you caught her?"
"That's the part that hurt the most, Your Honor. She turned and said, 'Well, look who's here! Old Blabbermouth. Now the whole neighborhood will know."

• •

After several months of married life, the glamour wore off and the young couple went to see a marriage counselor. After talking with the couple for awhile, the counselor suddenly swept the woman into his arms and kissed her passionately.

"Now," said the marriage counselor. "This is the treatment your wife needs....Monday, Thursday and

Saturday, at least."

"Okay," replied the husband. "I can bring here in here on Thursday and Saturday nights, but Monday is my bowling night."

•   •

Why can't you call the doctor? You aren't doing anything between contractions, are you?

•   •

The phone rang in the maternity ward and an excited voice on the other end said: "This is George Smith and I'm bringing my wife in . . . she's about to have a baby!"

"Calm down," replied the attendant. "Tell me, is this her first baby?"

"No," the voice replied, "this is her husband."

•   •

Buck: I'll be a bachelor for the next two weeks.

Ken: How is that?

Buck: My wife is going home to spend two weeks with her mother. She does this once a year. It's sort of a refresher course in nagging.

•   •

When you tell your wife to hurry and get ready for the party and she says I won't be a minute....she is usually right.

•   •

A lady was complaining to her husband about the ill manners of a friend who had just left. "If that woman yawned once while I was talking, she yawned ten times."

Maybe she wasn't yawning, dear," replied the husband. "Perhaps she was trying to say something."

•   •

Marriage is a legalized method of suppressing freedom of speech.

• •

A happy marriage is when a couple is as deeply in love as they are in debt.

• •

Some people marry for love, some for money, but most of them for only a short time.

• •

Epitaph seen on a stone in a country cemetary:
HERE LIES MY DARLING HUSBAND WALTER. MAY HE REST IN PEACE....UNTIL WE MEET AGAIN.

• •

Dave says he got married because he was tired of going to the laundromat, eating in restaurants and wearing socks with holes in them.
Jim says he got divorced for the same reasons.

• •

Lawyer: You say you want to get a divorce on the grounds that your husband is careless about his appearance?
Client: Yes, he hasn't appeared for almost five years now.

• •

A man was driving an auto with his wife in the back seat and stalled his car on the railroad tracks as the train was approaching.
His wife screamed: "Go on! Go on!"
"You've been driving all day from the back seat. I've got my end across....now see what you can do with your end."

• •

I take my wife out every night, but she keeps finding her way home.

• •

"I was married twice," explained the man, "and I'll never marry again. My first wife died eating poisonous mushrooms, and my second died of a fractured skull."
"That's a shame," said his friend. "How did it happen?"
"She wouldn't eat her mushrooms."

• •

My wife talks to her plants for three hours every day. I once asked a geranium, "How do you stand it?"
The geranium replied, "Who listens?"

• •

Melba: You'll never know what I went through to buy you your birthday present.
Ken: Come on, tell me.
Melba: All right....Your pockets.

• •

Buck: Did she make him a good wife?
Jack: Not exactly; but she's making him a good husband.

• •

He: By the way, do you remember the time I made such an idiot out of myself?
She: Which time?

• •

Groom: It seems to me, my dear, that there is something with this cake.
Bride: That shows what you know about it. The cook book says it's perfectly delicious.

• •

"John, John," whispered an alarmed wife, poking her sleeping husband in the ribs. "Wake up, John; there are burglars in the pantry and they're eating all my pies."

"Well, what do we care," mumbled John, rolling over, "so long as they don't die in the house?"

• •

After a long, boring evening with some neighbors the husband turned to his wife and said, "We had better go to bed, these people might want to go home."

• •

I know a couple who are so concerned with their health that whenever they have an arguement the wife jogs home to mother.

• •

A yawn is nature's way of letting a Husband open his mouth.

• •

Why shouldn't women have cleaner minds than men....note how often they change them.

• •

Linda: Darling . . . you know that cake you asked me to bake for you . . . well, the dog ate it.
Jack: That's okay, dear, don't cry . . . I'll buy another dog!

• •

A light passenger car driven by a farmer collided with a heavily loaded freight truck. All occupants of the car were shaken up, and the farmer's wife had her thumb cut off.

A few hours after she was discharged from the hospital, the claims adjuster for the trucking company called at her home.

She suggested a settlement figure and the adjuster turned purple with rage.

Madam," he exploded, "can't you see that your claim for fifty thousand dollars for a single digit is ridiculous."

"Maybe you think so," she explained, "but that was no ordinary thumb. It was the one I kept my husband under!"

• •

Bufe: Is your wife having any success in learning to drive the car?
Jay: Well, the road is beginning to turn when she does.

• •

Joe: The man who married Gwendolyn got a prize.
Moe: Yeah, for valor.

• •

Chairman: "Congratulations, my boy, congratulations on your typical married man's speech!"

• •

Ken: You accuse me of reckless extravagance. When did I ever make a useless purchase?
Melba: Why, there's that fire extinguisher you bought a year ago. We've never used it once.

• •

He: I'd love to be married to you some day.
She: All right, I'll put you on my wedding list.

• •

Nancy: Anything new in the paper today, Jim?
Jim: No, my dear....just the same old things, only happening to different people.

• •

Jan: Wake up, John, there's a burglar going through your pants pockets.
John: Oh, you two just fight it out between yourselves.

• •

BILL: Boy, if I had a wife like yours, I'd stay home every night in the week.
Bob: I'll say you would, or get your neck broken.

• •

Wife: You're lazy, you're worthless, you're bad-tempered, you're shiftless, you're a liar.
Husband: Well, my dear, no man is perfect.

• •

Speaking of marriage, the guy who coined the word "altar" must have been an Englishman who dropped his h's.

• •

Groom: What's wrong with this cake, dear? It tastes kind of gritty.
Bride: Don't be silly, darling. The recipe calls for three whole eggs and I guess I didn't get the shells beaten up fine enough.

• •

Wife to husband, "You'd better get up and go see why the baby's not crying."

• •

She: Doesn't the bride look stunning?
He: Yeah, doesn't the groom look stunned?

• •

Pam: You know, dear, Wayne doesn't seem to be as well dressed as he was when you married him.
Marilyn: That's funny. I'm sure it's the same suit.

• •

84

A good husband is one who feels in his pockets every time he passes a mail box.

• •

Pam: My husband is an efficiency expert in a large office.
Rosie: What does an efficiency expert do?
Pam: Well, if we women did it, they'd call it nagging.

• •

Herein lies the difference between the sexes: when a couple is supposed to go somewhere, the woman's first thought is: "What shall I wear?" and the man's: "How can I get out of it?"

• •

The meek little man approached a policeman on the street corner.
"Excuse me, officer," he said, "but I've been waiting here for my wife for over an hour. Would be kind enough to order me to move on?"

• •

Two ladies stopped to look at a bookstore display. "There's a book on HOW TO TORTURE YOUR HUS-BAND," said one.
"I don't need that," the other replied. "I have a system of my own."

• •

Marriage is the only known example of the happy meeting of the immovable object and the irresistible force.

• •

I am quite sure that marriage is the alliance of two people, one of whom never remembers birthdays and the other never forgets them.

• •

Bumper sticker: BEWARE OF SUDDEN STOPS....
TEACHING WIFE TO DRIVE.

• •

Dave: What is the greatest water power known to man?
Rich: Woman's tears.

• •

When my wife wants something she uses sign language. She always signs for this and signs for that.

• •

Becky: (admiring her engagement ring) There's nothing in the world harder than a diamond, is there?
Dave: Yes, sweetheart....keeping up the installment payments on it.

• •

The oyster is not the only one who has a crab for a mate.

• •

Melba: I can't decide whether to go to a palmist or to a mind-reader.
Ken: Go to a palmist. It's obvious that you have a palm.

• •

Nowadays, a couple marries and the first thing you know they have a little divorce.

• •

Sharon: Does your husband kick about the meals?
Esther: No, what he kicks about is having to get them.

• •

Martha: Is your husband a bookworm?
Roberta: No, just an ordinary one

• •

Boy: Do you know, Dad, that in some parts of Africa a man doesn't know his wife until he marries her?
Dad: Why single out Africa?

• •

Buck: But you must admit that men have better judgment than women.
Nancy: Oh, yes....you married me, and I you.

• •

Myrlene: How do you like the potato salad, dear?
Don: Delicious! Did you buy it yourself?

• •

Glen: I was hypnotized last week.
Rich: What's "hypnotized" mean?
Glen: Why, to hypnotize is to get a man in your power, and make him do whatever you want.
Rich: That's not hypnotism, that's marriage.

• •

"Did he take his misfortunes like a man?"
"Precisely. He laid the blame on his wife."

• •

Linda: I made this pudding all by myself.
Jack: Splendid! But who helped you lift it out of the oven?

• •

Ken: I slept like a log.
Melba: Yes, I heard the sawmill.

• •

"Now," said the prosecutor, "remember, you have sworn to tell the truth. Tell the jury just why you shot your husband with a bow and arrow."
"I didn't want to wake the children."

• •

A couple was celebrating their Golden Wedding Anniversary. Their domestic tranquility had long been the talk of the town. A local newspaper reporter was inquiring as to the secret of their long and happy marriage.

"Well, it dates back to our honeymoon," explained the lady. "We visited the Grand Canyon and took a trip down to the bottom of the canyon by pack mule. We hadn't gone too far when my husband's mule stumbled. He took him by the ears, shook him vigorously and said 'That's once.' We proceded a little farther when the mule stumbled again. Once more my husband took him by the ears, shook him even more vigorously and said, 'That's twice.' We hadn't gone a half mile when the mule stumbled a third time. My husband promptly removed a revolver from his pocket and shot him. I started to protest over his treatment of the mule when he grabbed me by the ears, shook me vigorously and said 'That's once.'"

TELEVISION

Before deciding to retire, stay home for a week and watch daytime TV shows.

●　　　●

Someone has suggested a TV series about a wealthy sheik and his many sons . . . to be called "OIL IN THE FAMILY."

●　　　●

Watch the television news and we find our highways aren't safe, our streets aren't safe, our parks aren't safe....but under our arms we've got complete protection.

●　　　●

Thanks to television, children now have seen more 1932 movies than their parents.

• •

Television announcer: "For those of you who sneaked into the kitchen during the sponsor's message, I'll repeat it now."

• •

"Your friend Rich seemed to be the life of the party."
"Yes, he was the only one who could talk louder than the TV."

• •

Announcer: "And now for all the news that happened during the last commercial...."

• •

The good guys always win on every TV show except the evening news.

• •

The quickest way to get a doctor or a policeman is to turn on your television set.

MONEY TALKS

Money talks . . . it says goodby.

• •

If you don't understand why Uncle Sam wears such a tall hat, you will when he passes it around.

• •

Tim: When I arrived in this country, I didn't even have any pockets to put a dime in.
Jim: How old were you?
Tim: I was born here.

• •

There's one advantage in being poor . . . it's very inexpensive.

• •

"What kind of work do you do?"
"I work for the Bureau of Internal Revenue."
"Doesn't everybody?"

• •

His monthly salary runs into five figures . . . his wife and four daughters.

• •

A bank is just a place where you keep the government's money until the tax man asks for it!

• •

Few of us can stand prosperity. Another man's, I mean.

• •

Two can live as cheap as one . . . they usually have to.

• •

The principle export of the United States is money.

• •

The thing that keeps men broke is not the wolf at the door but the silver fox in the window.

• •

A successful man is one who makes more money than his wife can spend. A successful woman is one who can find such a man.

• •

"Remember on our vacation when we spent money like there was no tomorrow? Well, it's tomorrow."

• •

A young husband who had agreed to buy a vacuum cleaner was disturbed when he found that his wife had ordered the deluxe model instead of the standard.

"But, dear," his wife explained, "it won't cost any more. All we have to do is pay a little longer."

•   •

Money is not the measure of man, but it is often the means of finding out how small he is.

•   •

A schoolboy was making a speech about the national debt: "It is too bad that future generations cannot be here at this time," he said, "to see the magnificent things we are doing with their money."

•   •

Sharon: Is your husband tight with money?
Esther: Is he? Every time he takes a penny out of his pocket Lincoln blinks at the light.

•   •

Randy: The way those people flaunt their money really makes me ill.
Bufe: Sour grapes always did have that effect.

•   •

The men were arguing as to who was the greatest inventor. One said Stephenson, who invented the locomotive. Another declared it was the man who invented the compass. Another contended for Edison. Still another for the Wright brothers.

Finally one of them turned to a little man who had remained silent:

"Who do you think?"

"Well," he said, with a hopeful smile, "the man who invented interest was no slouch."

•   •

A college boy wrote his father: "I can't understand how you can call yourself a kind parent when you haven't sent me a check in two months. What sort of kindness is that?"

The father replied: "Son, that's called unremitting kindness."

•   •

The easiest way to find something lost around the house is to buy a replacement.

•   •

Inflation has changed things. Now one can live as cheaply as two used to.

•   •

Wife to husband: "Well, at last I have a budget that works . . . and it was just a simple matter of ignoring Miscellaneous."

•   •

Living on a budget is the same as living beyond your means, except that you have a record of it.

•   •

A man buying meat looked at his bill and exclaimed, "No, no . . . you've got it wrong! I ordered a rolled roast, not a Rolls-Royce."

•   •

Some folks call their bank to get their balance. I just shake mine.

•   •

April is always a difficult month for Americans. Even if your ship comes in, the I.R.S. is right there to help you unload it.

•   •

Nowadays when someone asks, "What's up?" the answer is "Everything."

• •

Gas prices are so high, when I pulled into a station this morning and asked for a dollar's worth . . . the attendant dabbed some behind my ears.

• •

IRS agent to taxpayer: "I'm afraid we can't allow you to deduct last year's tax as a bad investment."

• •

Customer to employee at credit desk: "Social Security number, driver's license number, account number . . . don't you want to know my name?"

• •

The Federal Government worries about the growing number of unemployed; but business executives have the even greater worry of the growing number of unemployed still on the payroll.

• •

A modern day Rip Van Winkle slept for 20 years. Upon awaking he immediately called his broker.

"What's the stock market done the past 20 years?" he inquired.

With the aid of a computer his broker soon was able to report that his 100 shares of A.T.&T. were now worth $9.5 million, his 100 shares of General Motors worth $7.9 million, and his oil holding had increased to $19 million.

"Great!" Rip exclaimed, "I'm rich!"

At which point the telephone operator interrupted and said, "Your three minutes are up, sir. Would you please deposit a million dollars?"

• •

The U.S.A. is the only country where a housewife hires a woman to do her cleaning so she can do volunteer work at the day nursery where the cleaning woman leaves her child.

• •

Nowadays two can live as cheaply as one if both are working.

• •

Credit Manager: Do you have any money in the bank?
Loan Applicant: Certainly.
Credit Manager: How much?
Loan Applicant: I don't know. I haven't shaken it lately.

• •

Grandpa framed the first dollar he ever made in a 10c picture frame. Today the frame is worth a dollar and the dollar is worth 10c.

• •

Why do we spend five thousand dollars on a school bus to haul our children one mile, and then build a million dollar gymnasium for them to get exercise?

• •

Modern man is one who drives a mortgaged car down a bond financed highway using a credit card for gasoline.

• •

A loan company having trouble making a collection finally wrote the delinquent: "Dear Mr. Phillips: What would your neighbors think if we came to your place and repossessed your car?"

• •

Motorist to service-station attendant: "Just ten dollars' worth. I'm in a hurry."

• •

One small jack can lift a car, but it takes a lot of jack to keep it up.

• •

Don't put off until tomorrow what you should do today. If you do there will probably be a higher tax on it.

• •

Strange that men call money "dough." Dough sticks to your fingers.

• •

One reason the dollar won't do as much for anyone as it used to is the fact that no one will do as much for a dollar as they used to.

• •

Behind every successful man is a representative of the Internal Revenue Service.

• •

Probably the world's greatest humorist was the man who named them "easy payments."

• •

You're an old timer if you can remember when a family was considered shiftless if they lived from payday to payday. Now they're considered excellent financial managers if they can.

• •

The height of irony is to give a father a billfold for Christmas.

• •

Inflation marches on, making it possible for people in all walks of life to live in more expensive neighborhoods without ever moving.

• •

Running into debt isn't so bad. It's running into creditors that hurts.

• •

It's becoming more and more difficult to support the government in the style to which it has become accustomed.

THOUGHT STOPPERS

There are usually two sides to every argument but no end.

• •

If you think no evil, see no evil, and hear no evil, the chances are that you'll never write a best-selling novel.

• •

Never pick a quarrel even when it is ripe.

• •

Why does a woman say she's been shopping when she hasn't bought a thing?

• •

It has now been proven beyond a doubt that smoking is the major cause of statistics.

• •

Another way to make your new car's finish last is always to park it between new cars.

• •

The supermarket is where you spend 30 minutes hunting for instant coffee.

• •

All of us are experts at practicing virtue at a distance.

• •

If there's anything in evolution, Americanism should in time develop a very strong trigger finger.

• •

Those who censor the modern bathing-suit have scant reason for doing so.

• •

A sharp nose indicates curiosity. A flattened nose indicates too much curiosity.

• •

Many a man thinks he has an open mind when it's merely vacant.

• •

The only people who listen to both sides of an argument are the neighbors.

• •

A true gentleman is a man who knows how to play the bagpipe . . . but doesn't.

• •

You are getting old when your back goes out more often than you do.

• •

A man who sits in a swamp all day waiting to shoot a duck will kick if his wife has dinner ten minutes late.

• •

If at first you don't succeed, you'll get a lot of unsolicited advice.

• •

The more you say, the less people remember.

• •

Worry is like a rocking chair. It gives you something to do but it doesn't get you any place.

• •

People who live in glass houses might as well answer the doorbell.

• •

You can always tell when a man's well-informed. His views are pretty much like your own.

• •

Why is it the loudest snorer is always the first one to get to sleep?

• •

It's nice to see people with plenty of get-up-and-go, especially if some of them are visiting you.

• •

The trouble with being a good sport is, you have to lose to prove it.

• •

Many people's tombstones should read: "Died at 30. Buried at 60."

• •

A girdle is a device to keep an unfortunate situation from spreading.

• •

There isn't anything can be sliced so thin that it has only one side.

•   •

Sadness hears the clock strike every hour; happiness forgets the day of the month.

•   •

Remember the steam kettle . . . although up to its neck in hot water, it continues to sing.

•   •

When a man gets to the top everybody is willing to give him a boost.

•   •

A telephone pole never hits a motor car except in self-defense.

•   •

Today is the tomorrow you worried about yesterday.

•   •

Then there was the glass blower who inhaled . . . and got a pane in his stomach.

•   •

If at first you don't succeed, try looking in the wastebasket for the directions.

•   •

Who overcomes by force hath overcome but half his foe.

•   •

A conference is just an admission that you want somebody to join you in your troubles.

•   •

To be born a gentleman is an accident; to die one, an achievement.

. .

There is a growing sentiment that the national flower should be a concrete cloverleaf.

. .

Drive carefully. Why die in perfect health?

. .

For that run-down feeling . . . try jay-walking.

. .

Social tact is making your company feel at home even though you wish they were.

. .

Success is relative. The more success, the more relatives.

. .

Nothing is more exasperating than getting behind a guy in the lane who is observing the speed limit.

. .

The only fellow whose troubles are all behind him is a school bus driver.

. .

The real problem of leisure time is how to keep others from using yours.

. .

Never try to make anyone like yourself . . . you know, and God knows, that one of you is enough.

. .

Nostalgia isn't what it used to be.

. .

There's no point in burying a hatchet if you're going to put up a marker on the site.

• •

The trouble with opportunity is that it's always more recognizable going than coming.

• •

Tact is the ability to close one's mouth before someone else wants to do it.

• •

The man who thinks he knows it all is a pain in the neck to those of us who really do.

• •

Experience is the thing you have left when everything else is gone.

• •

A tactless person is someone who says what everyone else is thinking.

• •

If you can't get away for a vacation, just tip every third person you meet and you'll get the same effect.

• •

Life's briefest moment is the time between reading the sign on the freeway and realizing you just missed your exit.

• •

You're reaching middle age when it takes longer to rest up than it did to get tired.

• •

If you're not big enough to stand criticism, you're too small to be praised.

• •

No matter how busy people are, they are never too busy to stop and talk about how busy they are.

•   •

There's nothing like looking at vacation pictures to put guests in a traveling mood.

WINDY DAZE

Public speaking is the art of diluting a two-minute idea with a two-hour vocabulary.

•   •

The weaker the argument the stronger the words.

•   •

It is always dullest just before the yawn.

•   •

In general those who have nothing to say contrive to spend the longest time in doing it.

•   •

A noted American journalist on a trip to China was asked to speak before a Chinese audience. He accepted the invitation. He was about half through his speech when he noted a Chinese in a corner was writing on a blackboard. He became interested and as he spoke he watched the writer who was writing in Chinese. The writer wrote less and less and finally stopped completely. When he had finished speaking, the journalist asked the chairman what the writer had been doing.

"Why," said the chairman, "he was interpreting your speech for the benefit of the members of the audience who do not understand English."

"But," said the speaker, "for the last twenty

minutes he did not put anything down."

"Oh," said the chairman, "he was only writing the ideas on the blackboard."

· · ·

A long-winded speaker had been droning for an hour with reference to his trip to the Grand Canyon. "There I stood, with the great canyon yawning in front of me."

A voice from the back yelled, "I bet the canyon was yawning before you got there."

· · ·

The best ingredient in the recipe of public speaking is the shortening.

· · ·

Everything that could be done to make the great unemployed meeting a success had been accomplished. A large hall and a good speaker had been engaged. When the latter arrived, he seemed to be in a crabby frame of mind. Looking around, he beckoned the chairman.

"I would like to have a glass of water on my table, if you please," he said.

"To drink?" was the chairman's question.

"Oh, no," was the sarcastic retort, "when I've been speaking a half hour, I do a high dive."

· · ·

Oratory: the art of making deep noises from the chest sound like important messages from the brain.

· · ·

A toastmaster is a man who eats a meal he doesn't want so he can get up and tell a lot of stories he doesn't remember to people who've already heard them.

· · ·

Another form of wastefulness is expenditure of words beyond the income of ideas.

• •

Most of us know how to say nothing . . . few of us know when.

• •

When a speaker says, "Well, to make a long story short," it's too late.

• •

A chauffer-driven Cadillac pulled up in front of our auditorium . . . stopped with a jerk . . . and out came our speaker of the evening.

• •

After a great host of boring speakers had spoken, the last speaker rose to the platform clutching a bulky, prepared speech. The guest could hardly conceal their restlessness. However, he made many friends when he said, "Friends, it's so late I've decided just to mail each of you a copy of this speech." Then he bowed and sat down.

• •

"Thank you for the privilege of speaking to you in this magnificent auditorium. You know the meaning of the word 'auditorium,' don't you? It is derived from two Latin words . . . audio, to hear, and taurus, the bull."

• •

One of the pitfalls of having political speeches ghost-written was seen when a governor began to read a speech containing, he said, "One of my favorite stories."

It turned out that he had never heard the story before. He began laughing so hard that his glasses fell off and broke and he was unable to finish the rest of the speech.

• •

In making a good speech it is all right to have a train of thought just as long as you make sure you also have a terminal.

• •

Veteran speakers usually gesture vigorously and walk around and around. They say a moving target is harder to hit.

• •

After the dinner is over,
    After the waiters have gone,
After the coffee and mint-drops,
    After the very last song;
Then come the speeches and laughter,
    And we settle ourselves for a coke,
In the hope that one of the speakers
    Will tell us a really good joke.

• •

A speaker heard some hissing coming from his audience. He said, "There are only three things that hiss . . . a goose, a snake and a fool. Come forth and be identified."

• •

After a speaker had talked loud and long he asked the audience if there were any questions. A hand shot up. The speaker nodded.
    "What time is it?" the listener inquired.

• •

Sometimes the difference between a good speaker and a poor speaker is a comfortable nap.

• •

I will conclude with the story about the little boy in an anatomy class, who was asked to describe the spine. "It's a long, grisly kind of bone," he said. "The head rests on the top. At the other end . . . well, that's where I sit down!" (And Sit Down)

• •

Thank you for your wonderful reception, which I so richly deserve and so seldom get.

• •

Applause before a speaker begins his talk is an act of faith.

Applause during the speech is an act of hope.

Applause after he has concluded is an act of charity.

• •

Speak when you are angry and you'll make the best speech you'll ever regret.

HOARSE LAUGHS

A barber was cutting a crop of long hair off a young man and asked, "Were you in the navy once?"

"Yes," replied the young man. "How did you know?"

"I just found your cap," replied the barber.

• •

An undertaker telegraphed to a man that his mother-in-law had died and asked whether he should bury, embalm or cremate her. The man replied, "All three. Take no chances."

• •

The mother was having a hard time getting her son to go to school in the morning.

"Nobody likes me in school," he complained. "The teachers don't like me, the kids don't like me, the superintendent wants to transfer me, the bus drivers hate me, the school board wants me to drop out and the custodians have it in for me. I don't want to go to school."

"But you have to go to school," countered his mother. "You are healthy, you have a lot to learn, you have something to offer others, you are a leader. And besides, you are 45 years old and you are the principal."

• •

It's wonderful how the movies have progressed over the years. First there were silent pictures, then talkies, and now most of them smell.

• •

People are strange. Why is it a man will be too scared to visit his dentist, but will race a locomotive to a crossing?

• •

Each man must decide whether he wants to be his own self or a model of someone else. But before deciding remember, the dictionary defines a model as "a small imitation of the real thing."

• •

Most freeways have three lanes . . . a left lane, a right lane and the lane you're trapped in when you see your exit.

• •

Elephants live longer than people, according to a book we read. Maybe that's because they never worry about trying to lose weight.

• •

There are two types of leaders . . . those interested in the flock, and those interested in the fleece.

• •

A rather frugal gentleman was becoming increasingly hard of hearing, but decided a hearing aid was too expensive so he wrapped an ordinary piece of wire around his ear. "Do you hear better now with that wire around your ear?" asked a friend.

"Not a bit," came the reply, "but everybody talks louder."

• •

Randy: This clock will run 30 days without winding.
Jay: That's great. How long will it run if you wind it?

• •

Before boarding a plane, a man took out an accident policy for $100,000, then on his way to the boarding gate he stepped on a weight and fortune scale.

He was taken back a bit when he discovered his fortune card read, "Your recent investment will soon pay off."

• •

An executive was interviewing a lady applicant and after she handed him her filled-out form he remarked, "I see your birthday is April 17, what year?"

"Every year," she replied.

• •

Grandpa proudly announced to his family that he was going to get married again.

"I've been a widower long enough," he said. "I've picked me out another wife."

"Who are you going to marry?" asked his brother.

"Bob Vernon's daughter."

"But she's only 19," protested the brother. "Imagine a man your age . . . 88 . . . marrying a girl only 19 years old!"

"What's wrong with that?" inquired the old man. "That's exactly the same age my first wife was when I married her and you didn't say anything."

• •

One advantage to advancing years is that you know a lot more about being young than teen-agers know about being old.

• •

A bachelor kept a cat for companionship, and loved his cat more than life. He was planning a trip to England and entrusted the cat to his brother's care.

As soon as he arrived in England he called his brother. "How is my cat?" he asked.

"Your cat is dead," came the reply.

"Oh my," he exclaimed. "Did you have to tell me that way?"

"How else can I tell you your cat's dead?" inquired the brother.

"You should have led me up to it gradually," said the bachelor. "For example, when I called tonight you could have told me my cat was on the roof, but the Fire Department is getting it down. When I called tomorrow night, you could have told me they dropped him and broke his back, but a fine surgeon is doing all he can for him. Then, when I called the third night, you could have told me the surgeon did all he could but my cat passed away. That way it wouldn't have been such a shock.

"By the way," he continued, "how's Mother?"

"Mother?" came the reply. "Oh, she's up on the roof, but the Fire Department is getting her down."

• •

Sign on the back of a lumbering truck on a mountain highway: WE MAY BE SLOW, BUT WE'RE AHEAD OF YOU.

• •

When I asked a friend the secret of his popularity, he attributed it to one particular word. "Years ago," he said, "upon hearing a statement with which I disagreed, I used to say 'baloney' and people avoided me like the plague. Now I substitute 'amazing' for 'baloney,' and my phone keeps ringing with invitations."

• •

Sign above umbrellas and rain apparel: THUNDER WEAR.

• •

One trouble with developing speed reading skills is that by the time you realize a book is boring you've already finished it.

• •

A Texas rancher was visiting an Iowa farm. The Iowa farmer was justly proud of his 200 acres of rich, productive land.

"Is this your whole farm?" the Texan asked. "Why back in Texas I get in my car at 5:00 in the morning, and I drive and drive all day. At dusk I just reach the other end of my ranch."

The Iowa farmer thought a while and replied, "I used to have a car like that too."

• •

A lady engaged in washing her upstairs windows leaned out too far and fell, landing squarely in a garbage can. A passing Chinese gentleman looked, shrugged, and said, "Amelicans velly wasteful. Woman good for ten years yet.

• •

When it comes to gardening, there's no better labor-saving device than a bad back.

• •

At the conclusion of his lecture an explorer just back from South America was asked if it were true that wild animals wouldn't harm a person carrying a flaming torch. "That depends," answered the explorer, "entirely upon how fast you carry it."

• •

A man rushed into a drug store and asked a pharmacist for something to stop hiccups. The druggist poured a glass of water and threw it into the man's face.

"Why did you do that?" the man exploded angrily.

"Well, you don't have hiccups now, do you?"

"No!" shouted the customer. "But my wife out in the car still has!"

• •

Two Indians were driving along at 80 miles an hour.

1st Indian: I think we're getting near the reservation.

2nd Indian: Why?

1st Indian: We're hitting more Indians.

• •

Bufe: Did your watch stop when it dropped on the floor?

Ken: Sure! Did you think it would go through?

• •

Pam: Think of those Spaniards going 3,000 miles on a galleon!

Melba: You can't believe all you hear about those little foreign cars.

• •

Did you hear about the man who crossed a turkey with a centipede? On Thanksgiving, everybody got a drumstick.

• •

Did you hear about the man who crossed an octopus with a bale of straw and got a broom with eight handles?

• •

Did you hear about the man who crossed a carrier pigeon with a woodpecker so when he delivers the message, he can knock on the door?

• •

Martha: Did you give up anything during Lent?
Roberta: Yes. I gave up fifty dollars for a new Easter dress.

• •

The housemaid, tidying the stairs the morning after a reception, found lying there one of the solid silver teaspoons.

"My goodness gracious!" she exclaimed, as she retrieved the piece of silver. "Some one of the company had a hole in his pocket."

• •

Guide: This building has been here for over six hundred years. Not a stone has been touched, nothing changed, nothing replaced.
Tourist: They must have the same landlord as we have.

• •

A local newspaper had a very difficult time in reporting the death of one of the town members.

The first report said, "Brother Poure has gone to rust." They tried to correct the misprint the next day

112

and it came out, "Brother Poure has gone to roost."
Finally they tried a third time and the report stated,
"Brother Poure has gone to roast."

• •

Bob was exceptionally bald. Bill was prematurely
gray. One day these two met on the street and Bob
said, "Bill, you are certainly getting gray."

"Yes," said Bill, "but I'd rather be gray than bald
like you, especially since I learned the cause of both.
Scientists claim that the roots of the hair grow in
deeply and when they strike something gray the hair
naturally turns the same color. If the roots strike
nothing, the hair falls out."

"On the other hand," said Bob, "historians have
learned that all barbarians have hair, which seems to
prove that the less hair you have, the more civilized
you are."

• •

Melba: I notice by this article that men become
bald much more than women because of the intense
activity of their brains.
Ken: Yes, and I notice that women don't raise beards
because of the intense activity of their chins!

• •

"Sorry, sir, but I'm all out of wild ducks. I could let
you have a fine end of ham."

"Don't kid me. How could I go home and say I shot
an end of ham?"

• •

Bob: Don't be afraid of my dog. You know the old
proverb, "A barking dog never bites."
Rich: Yes, you know the proverb, and I know the
proverb, but does your dog know the proverb?

• •

A boy was taking a stroll through a cemetery and reading the inscriptions on tombstones. He came to one which declared: "Not dead, but sleeping."

After contemplating the phrase for a moment, and scratching his head, he exclaimed: "He sure ain't foolin' nobody but himself."

• •

Passenger: Porter, what about these shoes? One's black and one's tan!

Porter: Well, if it don't beat all! This is the second time today that's happened.

• •

Love should be behind every wedding, but not too far behind.

• •

About three weeks before an annual club dinner, a member received a letter from the club president, asking him to serve on the reception committee and be there at seven o'clock sharp. A scarlet ribbon marked RECEPTION COMMITTEE was enclosed. He hadn't meant to go. The dinners were usually a bore. But since he had been asked to be on the committee he decided to go.

By the time he arrived, almost all 800 members of the club were there, each wearing a scarlet ribbon marked RECEPTION COMMITTEE.

• •

Why must we have enough memory to recall to the tiniest detail what has happened to us, and not have enough to remember how many times we have told it to the same person?

• •

Two Americans, hunting in an African jungle, suddenly found themselves face to face with a very rare (and very hungry-looking) saber-toothed tiger.

"What'll we do?" quavered the first.

"I don't know about you," the second croaked, "but I'm starting right now to spread the news of this wonderful find throughout Africa!"

•   •

Mother rabbit to her small child: "A magician pulled you out of a hat . . . now stop asking questions."

•   •

Sharks with hands have been discovered in the South Seas. These, it is believed, were developed telling other fish how big the fellow was that got away.

•   •

During a seance, a medium was bringing people back from the other world. A ten-year-old kid was among those present. "I want to talk to Grandpa," he insisted.

"Quiet!" hushed the medium, quite annoyed.

"I want to talk to Grandpa," repeated the kid.

"Very well, little boy," said the medium, making a few hocus-pocus passes. "here he is."

"Grandpa," said the little boy, "what are you doing there? You ain't dead yet."

•   •

Jay: Why don't you sing a love song for us.
Randy: O.K., I'll sing 'Hold that Tiger.'
Jay: But, 'Hold that Tiger' isn't a love song.
Randy: It is to another tiger.

•   •

Pianist: I play by ear.
Companion: I listen the same way.

•   •

One of the greatest causes of world trouble is that ignorant people are so positive about things . . . and intelligent people are so full of doubts.

• •

A good many things are easier said than done . . . including wedding vows.

• •

A boy from New York was being led through the swamps of Georgia.

"Is it true," he asked, "that an alligator won't attack you if you carry a flashlight?"

"That depends," replied the guide, "on how fast you carry the flashlight."

• •

Every bride and groom would do well to remember that in wedding the we comes before the I.

• •

If you can keep your head when all those about you are losing theirs . . . perhaps it's because you just don't understand the situation.

• •

Brad: You look down-hearted. What are you worried about?

Charlie: My future.

Brad: What makes your future seem so hopeless?

Charlie: My past.

• •

The difference between an amateur and a professional athlete is that the latter is paid by check.

• •

Sign on the top of a high mountain: BE CAREFUL NOT TO FALL HERE. IT'S DANGEROUS. BUT IF YOU

DO FALL, REMEMBER TO LOOK TO THE LEFT. YOU
GET A WONDERFUL VIEW ON THAT SIDE.

• •

Dave: There are two sides to every question.
Rich: Yes, and there are two sides to a sheet of
flypaper, but it makes no difference to the fly which
side he chooses.

• •

"Don't leave in the middle of the play. I promise
there's a terrific kick in the next act," said the
manager of the theater.
  "Fine," was the retort. "Give it to the author."

• •

Don: I heard what you just said about me, and I'll
give you just five seconds to apologize!
Glen: And what happens if I don't apologize in five
seconds?
Don: Well, how much time would you like?

• •

The average man's life consists of twenty years of
having his mother ask him where he is going; forty
years of having his wife ask the same question; and
at the end, the mourners wonder too.

• •

I ran into a former neighbor and asked how our old
mutual landlord was doing. "He's the same," was the
answer. "He's letting me have my apartment done in
any color of my choice . . . but I have to pay for the
crayons."

• •

Actor: It looks like a poor house, tonight.
Manager: You're wrong. It's a poorhouse tomorrow.

• •

A man answered his doorbell and a friend walked in, followed by a very large dog. As they began talking, the dog knocked over a lamp and jumped up on the sofa with his muddy feet and began chewing on one of the pillows.

The outraged householder, unable to contain himself any longer, burst out, "Don't you think you should train your dog better?"

"My dog!" exclaimed the friend, surprised. "I thought it was your dog."

• •

An old European monastery is perched high on a 500-foot cliff. Visitors ride up in a big basket, pulled to the top with a ragged old rope.

Halfway up, a passenger nervously asked: "How often do you change the rope?"

The monk in charge replied: "Whenever the old one breaks."

• •

After his bride's first display of independence, the young husband said reproachfully: "Have you forgotten that you promised to obey' when we were married?"

"No," she retorted, "but there will be time enough for that when I see some of the worldly goods with which you promised to endow me!"

• •

A struggling author had called on a publisher about a manuscript he had submitted.

"This is quite well written, but my firm publishes works only be writers with well-known names," said the publisher.

"Splendid," said the author. "My name's Smith."

• •

A department store with computerized accounts sent

the following notice to delinquent customers: IF YOU DO NOT PAY YOUR BILL RIGHT AWAY, YOUR ACCOUNT WILL BE TURNED OVER TO A HUMAN.

• •

A famous author was asked by an ambitious would-be author to impart his magic formula for writing success. "It's not hard to write the funny stuff." said the famous author. "All you have to do is procure a pen and paper, and some ink, and then sit down and write it as it occurs to you."

"Yes, yes," the would-be writer prompted.

"The writing is not hard," he continued. "But the occurring . . . that, my friend, is the difficulty."

• •

Recipe for an editor:
Take a personal hatred of authors,
   Mix this with a fiendish delight
In refusing all efforts of genius
   And maiming all poets on sight.

• •

I take the view that if you cannot say what you have to say in twenty minutes, you should go away and write a book about it.

• •

Jack: Why does a black cow that eats green grass give white milk that makes yellow butter?
Linda: For the same reason that black raspberries are red when they are green.

• •

Asking a woman her age is like buying a used car: you know the speedometer has been turned back, but you don't know how far.

• •

Sign in a bookstore window: YOU CAN'T JUDGE A
BOOK BY ITS MOVIE

. .

It's always a good idea to kiss your children good
night . . . that is, if you don't mind waiting up until
they get home.

. .

Ken: There's nothing like getting up at five in the
morning, taking an ice-cold shower, and a five-mile
jog before breakfast.
Bob: How long have you been doing this?
Ken: I start tomorrow.

. .

Wouldn't it be wonderful if the designers of women's
bathing suits were put in charge of government
budgets?

. .

Mr. and Mrs. McKee, vacationing in Rome, were
being shown through the Colosseum.
  "Now, this room," said the guide, "is where the
slaves dressed to fight the lions."
  "But how does one dress to fight lions?" inquired
Mr. McKee.
  "Very slow-w-w-w-w-wly," replied the guide.

. .

Jan: Do you file your fingernails?
Dave: Naw, I just throw them away after I cut them.

. .

Lady: So you are on a submarine. What do you do?
Sailor: Oh, I run forward, ma'am, and hold her nose
when we want to take a dive.

. .

The trouble with the younger generation is that too many of us don't belong to it anymore.

• •

The first real cure for dandruff was invented by a Frenchman. He called it the guillotine.

• •

Rich: About that book I lent you last week . . .
Glen: Sorry, I just lent it to a friend. Did you want it back?
Rich: Not for myself, but the guy I borrowed it from says the owner is looking for it.

• •

The Little League coach called one of his players over to him and said he would like to explain some of the principles of sportsmanship

"We don't believe in temper tantrums, screaming at the umpires, using bad language or sulking when we lose. Do you understand what I am saying?"

The boy nodded.

"All right, then," said the coach. "Do you think you can explain it to your father jumping around over there in the stands?"

• •

As he was drilling a batch of recruits, the sergeant saw that one of them was marching out of step. Going to the man as they marched, he said sarcastically:

"Do you know they are all out of step except you?"

"What?" asked the recruit innocently.

"I said they are all out of step except you," repeated the sergeant.

"Well," was the retort, "you tell 'em. You're in charge."

• •

To discover whether an ostrich is male or female . . . tell it a joke.

If he laughs, it's a male.
If she laughs, it's a female.

•   •

Tourist: Good river for fish?
Fisherman: It must be. I can't persuade any to come out.

•   •

One day Ed met two old friends and invited them home for dinner. He lived on the twentieth floor of an apartment house. Today the elevators were all out of order and they would have to walk up. Ed said to his friends: "The climb won't seem so bad if we amuse ourselves as we climb. One of you sing songs, the other tell jokes, and I'll tell a sad, sad story." They climbed and climbed. When they reached the top, gasping, it was Ed's turn to tell his sad story. He did. "Gee," he said, feeling in his pockets, "know what? I left my doorkey downstairs in my car."

•   •

"The reason I climb mountains is . . . because they are there!"

"That's the reason everybody else goes around them!"